MznLnx

Missing Links Exam Preps

Exam Prep for

Government and Not-For-Profit Accounting: Concepts and Practices

Granof, 3rd Edition

The MznLnx Exam Prep is your link from the texbook and lecture to your exams.
The MznLnx Exam Preps are unauthorized and comprehensive reviews of your textbooks.

All material provided by MznLnx and Rico Publications (c) 2010
Textbook publishers and textbook authors do not particpate in or contribute to these reviews.

MznLnx

Rico
Publications

Exam Prep for Government and Not-For-Profit Accounting: Concepts and Practices
3rd Edition
Granof

Publisher: Raymond Houge
Assistant Editor: Michael Rouger
Text and Cover Designer: Lisa Buckner
Marketing Manager: Sara Swagger
Project Manager, Editorial Production: Jerry Emerson
Art Director: Vernon Lowerui

Product Manager: Dave Mason
Editorial Assitant: Rachel Guzmanji
Pedagogy: Debra Long
Cover Image: Jim Reed/Getty Images
Text and Cover Printer: City Printing, Inc.
Compositor: Media Mix, Inc.

(c) 2010 Rico Publications
ALL RIGHTS RESERVED. No part of this work
covered by the copyright may be reproduced or
used in any form or by an means--graphic, electronic,
or mechanical, including photocopying, recording,
taping, Web distribution, information storage, and
retrieval systems, or in any other manner--without the
written permission of the publisher.

Printed in the United States
ISBN:

For more information about our products, contact us at:
Dave.Mason@RicoPublications.com

For permission to use material from this text or
product, submit a request online to:
Dave.Mason@RicoPublications.com

Contents

CHAPTER 1
THE GOVERNMENT AND NOT-FOR-PROFIT ENVIRONMENT — 1

CHAPTER 2
FUND ACCOUNTING — 13

CHAPTER 3
ISSUES OF BUDGETING AND CONTROL — 17

CHAPTER 4
RECOGNIZING REVENUES IN GOVERNMENTAL FUNDS — 25

CHAPTER 5
RECOGNIZING EXPENDITURES IN GOVERNMENTAL FUNDS — 33

CHAPTER 6
ACCOUNTING FOR CAPITAL PROJECTS AND DEBT SERVICE — 40

CHAPTER 7
LONG-LIVED ASSETS AND INVESTMENTS IN MARKETABLE SECURITIES — 46

CHAPTER 8
LONG-TERM OBLIGATIONS — 53

CHAPTER 9
BUSINESS-TYPE ACTIVITIES — 63

CHAPTER 10
FIDUCIARY FUNDS AND PERMANENT FUNDS — 70

CHAPTER 11
ISSUES OF REPORTING, DISCLOSURE, AND FINANCIAL ANALYSIS — 76

CHAPTER 12
OTHER NOT-FOR-PROFIT ORGANIZATIONS — 80

CHAPTER 13
USING COST INFORMATION TO MANAGE AND CONTROL — 87

CHAPTER 14
MANAGING FOR RESULTS — 94

CHAPTER 15
AUDITING GOVERNMENTS AND NOT-FOR-PROFIT ORGANIZATIONS — 99

CHAPTER 16
FEDERAL GOVERNMENT ACCOUNTING — 104

ANSWER KEY — 111

TO THE STUDENT

COMPREHENSIVE

The *MznLnx* Exam Prep series is designed to help you pass your exams. Editors at MznLnx review your textbooks and then prepare these practice exams to help you master the textbook material. Unlike study guides, workbooks, and practice tests provided by the texbook publisher and textbook authors, *MznLnx* gives you **all** of the material in each chapter in exam form, not just samples, so you can be sure to nail your exam.

MECHANICAL

The MznLnx Exam Prep series creates exams that will help you learn the subject matter as well as test you on your understanding. Each question is designed to help you master the concept. Just working through the exams, you gain an understanding of the subject--its a simple mechanical process that produces success.

INTEGRATED STUDY GUIDE AND REVIEW

MznLnx is not just a set of exams designed to test you, its also a comprehensive review of the subject content. Each exam question is also a review of the concept, making sure that you will get the answer correct without having to go to other sources of material. You learn as you go! Its the easiest way to pass an exam.

HUMOR

Studying can be tedious and dry. MznLnx's instructional design includes moderate humor within the exam questions on occassion, to break the tedium and revitalize the brain

Chapter 1. THE GOVERNMENT AND NOT-FOR-PROFIT ENVIRONMENT 1

1. The _____ is the national, professional association of CPAs in the United States, with more than 330,000 members, including CPAs in business and industry, public practice, government, and education; student affiliates; and international associates. It sets ethical standards for the profession and U.S. auditing standards for audits of private companies; federal, state and local governments; and non-profit organizations.

Approximately 40% of its members are engaged in the practice of public accounting, in areas such as auditing, accounting, taxation, general business consulting, business valuation, personal financial planning and business technology.

- a. AIG
- b. ABC Television Network
- c. Other postemployment benefits
- d. American Institute of Certified Public Accountants

2. The _____ is a private, not-for-profit organization whose primary purpose is to develop generally accepted accounting principles (GAAP) within the United States in the public's interest. The Securities and Exchange Commission (SEC) designated the _____ as the organization responsible for setting accounting standards for public companies in the U.S. It was created in 1973, replacing the Accounting Principles Board and the Committee on Accounting Procedure of the American Institute of Certified Public Accountants. The _____'s mission is 'to establish and improve standards of financial accounting and reporting for the guidance and education of the public, including issuers, auditors, and users of financial information.'

The _____ is not a governmental body.

- a. Fannie Mae
- b. Governmental Accounting Standards Board
- c. Financial Accounting Standards Board
- d. Public company

3. _____ is an umbrella term which refers to the various accounting systems used by various public sector entities. In the United States, for instance, there are two levels of government which follow different accounting standards set forth by independent, private sector boards. At the federal level, the Federal Accounting Standards Advisory Board (FASAB) sets forth the accounting standards to follow.

- a. Product control
- b. Management accounting
- c. Nonassurance services
- d. Governmental Accounting

4. The _____ is currently the source of generally accepted accounting principles (GAAP) used by State and Local governments in the [[United States of America]]. As with most of the entities involved in creating GAAP in the United States, it is a private, non-governmental organization.

The _____ is subject to oversight by the Financial Accounting Foundation (FAF), which selects the members of the _____ and the Financial Accounting Standards Board, and funds both organizations.

- a. National Conference of Commissioners on Uniform State Laws
- b. Fannie Mae
- c. Governmental Accounting Standards Board
- d. Multinational corporation

5. _____ is the term used to refer to the standard framework of guidelines for financial accounting used in any given jurisdiction. _____ includes the standards, conventions, and rules accountants follow in recording and summarizing transactions, and in the preparation of financial statements.

Financial accounting information must be assembled and reported objectively.

a. General ledger
b. Long-term liabilities
c. Generally accepted accounting principles
d. Current asset

6. Project _____: The project _____ is a prediction of the costs associated with a particular company project. These costs include labor, materials, and other related expenses. The project _____ is often broken down into specific tasks, with task _____s assigned to each.

a. BMC Software, Inc.
b. BNSF Railway
c. 3M Company
d. Budget

7. The _____ is a federal agency within the legislative branch of the United States government. It is a government agency that provides economic data to Congress. It was created by the Congressional Budget and Impoundment Control Act of 1974.

a. Congressional Budget Office
b. General Accounting Office
c. BMC Software, Inc.
d. 3M Company

8. The _____ after Senator Harold Burton of Ohio and Senator Lister Hill of Alabama, is a United States federal law passed in 1946. This act responded to the first of Trumane;s proposals and was designed to provide federal grants and guaranteed loans to improve the physical plant of the natione;s hospital system. Money was designated to the states to achieve 4.5 beds per 1,000 people.

a. Lease
b. Tax patent
c. Hospital Survey and Construction Act
d. Model Code of Professional Responsibility

9. The term _____ usually refers to a company that is permitted to offer its registered securities (stock, bonds, etc.) for sale to the general public, typically through a stock exchange, or occasionally a company whose stock is traded over the counter (OTC) via market makers who use non-exchange quotation services.

The term '_____' may also refer to a company owned by the government.

a. Public Company
b. MicroStrategy
c. Professional association
d. Governmental Accounting Standards Board

10. The _____ (sometimes called 'Peekaboo') is a private-sector, non-profit corporation created by the Sarbanes-Oxley Act, a 2002 United States federal law, to oversee the auditors of public companies. Its stated purpose is to 'protect the interests of investors and further the public interest in the preparation of informative, fair, and independent audit reports'. Although a private entity, the _____ has many government-like regulatory functions, making it in some ways similar to the private Self Regulatory Organizations (SROs) that regulate stock markets and other aspects of the financial markets in the United States.

a. Financial Crimes Enforcement Network
b. Pension Benefit Guaranty Corporation
c. 3M Company
d. Public Company Accounting Oversight Board

Chapter 1. THE GOVERNMENT AND NOT-FOR-PROFIT ENVIRONMENT

11. _____ is the balance of the amounts of cash being received and paid by a business during a defined period of time, sometimes tied to a specific project. Measurement of _____ can be used

- to evaluate the state or performance of a business or project.
- to determine problems with liquidity. Being profitable does not necessarily mean being liquid. A company can fail because of a shortage of cash, even while profitable.
- to project rate of returns. The time of _____s into and out of projects are used as inputs to financial models such as internal rate of return, and net present value.
- to examine income or growth of a business when it is believed that accrual accounting concepts do not represent economic realities. Alternately, _____ can be used to 'validate' the net income generated by accrual accounting.

_____ as a generic term may be used differently depending on context, and certain _____ definitions may be adapted by analysts and users for their own uses. Common terms include operating _____ and free _____.

a. Controlling interest
b. Cash flow
c. Commercial paper
d. Flow-through entity

12. _____ is a company's financial statement that indicates how the revenue is transformed into the net income The purpose of the _____ is to show managers and investors whether the company made or lost money during the period being reported.

The important thing to remember about an _____ is that it represents a period of time.

a. AMEX
b. Income statement
c. AIG
d. ABC Television Network

13. _____ is a demonstration of a process -- such as a variable, term, or object -- relative in terms of the specific process or set of validation tests used to determine its presence and quantity. Properties described in this manner must be sufficiently accessible, so that persons other than the definer may independently measure or test for them at will. An _____ is generally designed to model a conceptual definition.

a. ABC Television Network
b. AMEX
c. AIG
d. Operational definition

14. A _____ is a pool of assets forming an independent legal entity that are bought with the contributions to a pension plan for the exclusive purpose of financing pension plan benefits.

_____s are important shareholders of listed and private companies. They are especially important to the stock market where large institutional investors like the Ontario Teachers' Pension Plan dominate.

a. Public offering
b. Limited liability company
c. Return on assets
d. Pension fund

15. A budget _____ occurs when an entity spends more money than it takes in. The opposite of a budget _____ is a budget surplus. Debt is essentially an accumulated flow of _____s.

4   *Chapter 1. THE GOVERNMENT AND NOT-FOR-PROFIT ENVIRONMENT*

    a. Deficit   b. Windfall profits tax
    c. Progressive tax   d. Land value taxation

16. The term _____ refers to government debt, expenditures and revenues, or to finance (particularly financial revenue) in general.

- _____ deficit is the budget deficit of federal or local government
- _____ policy is the discretionary spending of governments. Contrasts with monetary policy.
- _____ year and _____ quarter are reporting periods for firms and other agencies.

See also

- Procurator _____ and Crown Office and Procurator _____ Service

    a. Fiscal   b. Scientific Research and Experimental Development Tax Incentive Program
    c. Comparable   d. Swap

17. The _____ is a Cabinet-level office, and is the largest office within the Executive Office of the President of the United States (EOP.) It is an important conduit by which the White House oversees the activities of federal agencies. OMB is tasked with giving expert advice to senior White House officials on a range of topics relating to federal policy, management, legislative, regulatory, and budgetary issues.

    a. Office of Management and Budget   b. AT'T Wireless Services, Inc.
    c. Alaska Air Group   d. Analysis of variance

18. A _____ is any one of a variety of different systems, institutions, procedures, social relations and infrastructures whereby persons trade, and goods and services are exchanged, forming part of the economy. It is an arrangement that allows buyers and sellers to exchange things. _____s vary in size, range, geographic scale, location, types and variety of human communities, as well as the types of goods and services traded.

    a. Market Failure   b. Recession
    c. Perfect competition   d. Market

19. _____ is the price at which an asset would trade in a competitive Walrasian auction setting. _____ is often used interchangeably with open _____, fair value or fair _____, although these terms have distinct definitions in different standards, and may differ in some circumstances.

International Valuation Standards defines _____ as 'the estimated amount for which a property should exchange on the date of valuation between a willing buyer and a willing seller in an arme;s-length transaction after proper marketing wherein the parties had each acted knowledgeably, prudently, and without compulsion.'

_____ is a concept distinct from market price, which is e;the price at which one can transacte;, while _____ is e;the true underlying valuee; according to theoretical standards.

Chapter 1. THE GOVERNMENT AND NOT-FOR-PROFIT ENVIRONMENT

a. Segregated portfolio company
c. Sinking fund
b. Debtor
d. Market value

20. An _____ is a term used in behavioral economics to describe those types of behaviors that impose costs on a person in the long-run that are not taken into account when making decisions in the present. Classical Economics discourages government from creating legislation that targets internalities, because it is assumed that the consumer takes these personal costs into account when paying for the good that causes the _____. For example, cigarettes should be taxed because of the negative consumption externalities that they impose, such as second-hand smoke, not because the smoker harms him or herself by smoking.
   a. Internality
   c. Operating budget
   b. Authorised capital
   d. Inventory turnover ratio

21. A _____ is an administrative entity composed of a clearly defined territory and its population and commonly denotes a city, town or a small grouping of them. A _____ is typically governed by a mayor and a city council or municipal council.

The notion of _____ includes townships but is not restricted to them.

   a. 3M Company
   c. BNSF Railway
   b. Municipality
   d. BMC Software, Inc.

22. The word _____ indicates that a party, or proprietor, exercises private ownership, control or use over an item of property
   a. 3M Company
   c. BNSF Railway
   b. BMC Software, Inc.
   d. Proprietary

23. In economics, business, retail, and accounting, a _____ is the value of money that has been used up to produce something, and hence is not available for use anymore. In economics, a _____ is an alternative that is given up as a result of a decision. In business, the _____ may be one of acquisition, in which case the amount of money expended to acquire it is counted as _____.
   a. Cost allocation
   c. Cost
   b. Cost of quality
   d. Prime cost

24. In economics and finance, _____ is the change in total cost that arises when the quantity produced changes by one unit. It is the cost of producing one more unit of a good. Mathematically, the _____ function is expressed as the first derivative of the total cost (TC) function with respect to quantity (Q.)
   a. Cost accounting
   c. Marginal cost
   b. Cost of quality
   d. Variable cost

25. A _____ is a fungible, negotiable instrument representing financial value. they are broadly categorized into debt securities (such as banknotes, bonds and debentures), and equity securities; e.g., common stocks. The company or other entity issuing the _____ is called the issuer.
   a. Tracking stock
   c. Security
   b. BMC Software, Inc.
   d. 3M Company

Chapter 1. THE GOVERNMENT AND NOT-FOR-PROFIT ENVIRONMENT

26. _____ in the United States currently refers to the federal Old-Age, Survivors, and Disability Insurance (OASDI) program.

The original _____ Act and the current version of the Act, as amended encompass several social welfare and social insurance programs. The larger and better known programs are:

- Federal Old-Age, Survivors, and Disability Insurance
- Unemployment benefits
- Temporary Assistance for Needy Families
- Health Insurance for Aged and Disabled (Medicare)
- Grants to States for Medical Assistance Programs (Medicaid)
- State Children's Health Insurance Program (SCHIP)
- Supplemental Security Income (Social SecurityI)

U.S. _____ is a social insurance program funded through dedicated payroll taxes called Federal Insurance Contributions Act (FICA.) Tax deposits are formally entrusted to Federal Old-Age and Survivors Insurance Trust Fund, or Federal Disability Insurance Trust Fund, Federal Hospital Insurance Trust Fund or the Federal Supplementary Medical Insurance Trust Fund.

a. Price-to-sales ratio
b. Comparable
c. Sale
d. Social Security

27. The United States _____ is an independent agency of the United States federal government that administers Social Security, a social insurance program consisting of retirement, disability, and survivors' benefits. To qualify for these benefits, most American workers pay Social Security taxes on their earnings; future benefits are based on the employees' contributions.

The _____ was established by a law currently codified at 42 U.S.C.

a. Time value of money
b. Minority interest
c. Return on assets
d. Social Security Administration

28. An _____ is a practitioner of accountancy, which is the measurement, disclosure or provision of assurance about financial information that helps managers, investors, tax authorities and other decision makers make resource allocation decisions.

The word '_____' is derived from the French 'Compter' which took its origin from the Latin 'Computare'. The word was formerly written in English as 'Accomptant', but in process of time the word, which was always pronounced by dropping the 'p', became gradually changed both in pronunciation and in orthography to its present form.

a. AMEX
b. AIG
c. ABC Television Network
d. Accountant

Chapter 1. THE GOVERNMENT AND NOT-FOR-PROFIT ENVIRONMENT

29. The _____ of a company or public agency is the corporate officer primarily responsible for managing the financial risks of the business or agency. This officer is also responsible for financial planning and record-keeping, as well as financial reporting to higher management. (In recent years, however, the role has expanded to encompass communicating financial performance and forecasts to the analyst community.)
    a. Chief executive officer
    b. Merck ' Co., Inc.
    c. NASDAQ
    d. Chief Financial Officer

30. The _____ signed into law by President George H.W. Bush on November 15, 1990, is a United States federal law intended to improve the government's financial management, outlining standards of financial performance and disclosure. Among other measures, the Office of Management and Budget (OMB) was given greater authority over federal financial management. For each of 23 federal departments and agencies, the position of chief financial officer was created.
    a. Bylaw
    b. Chief Financial Officers Act of 1990
    c. Jenkins Committee
    d. Scottish Poor Laws

31. The _____ was established as the _____ by the Budget and Accounting Act of 1921 (Pub.L. 67-13, 42 Stat. 20, June 10, 1921.)
    a. 3M Company
    b. GAO
    c. General Accounting Office
    d. BMC Software, Inc.

32. The _____ is the global organization for the accountancy profession. IFAC has 157 member bodies and associates in 123 countries and jurisdictions, representing more than 2.5 million accountants employed in public practice, industry and commerce, government, and academe. The organization, through its independent standard-setting boards, establishes international standards on ethics,auditing and assurance, education, and public sector accounting.
    a. International Accounting Standards Committee
    b. Emerging technologies
    c. International Federation of Accountants
    d. American Payroll Association

33. A _____ is a party (e.g. person, organization, company, or government) that has a claim to the services of a second party. It is a person or institution to whom money is owed. The first party, in general, has provided some property or service to the second party under the assumption (usually enforced by contract) that the second party will return an equivalent property or service.
    a. Payback period
    b. Treasury company
    c. Par value
    d. Creditor

34. Employment is a contract between two parties, one being the employer and the other being the _____. An _____ may be defined as: 'A person in the service of another under any contract of hire, express or implied, oral or written, where the employer has the power or right to control and direct the _____ in the material details of how the work is to be performed.' Black's Law Dictionary page 471 (5th ed. 1979).
    a. AIG
    b. AMEX
    c. ABC Television Network
    d. Employee

35. _____ are formal records of a business' financial activities.

In British English, including United Kingdom company law, _____ are often referred to as accounts, although the term _____ is also used, particularly by accountants.

_____ provide an overview of a business' financial condition in both short and long term.

Chapter 1. THE GOVERNMENT AND NOT-FOR-PROFIT ENVIRONMENT

a. 3M Company
b. Statement of retained earnings
c. Financial statements
d. Notes to the financial statements

36. _____ is an accounting system often used by nonprofit organizations and by the public sector. According to StartHereGoPlaces, _____ is a '[m]ethod of accounting and presentation whereby assets and liabilities are grouped according to the purpose for which they are to be used.'

_____ serves any nonprofit organization or the public sector. These organizations have a need for special reporting to financial statements users that show how money is spent, rather than how much profit was earned.

a. Refunding
b. Liquidating dividend
c. Replacement cost
d. Fund accounting

37. To tax is to impose a financial charge or other levy upon a _____ by a state or the functional equivalent of a state.

Taxes are also imposed by many subnational entities. Taxes consist of direct tax or indirect tax, and may be paid in money or as its labour equivalent (often but not always unpaid.)

a. Taxpayer
b. State tax levels
c. Tax avoidance
d. Federal Unemployment Tax Act

38. _____ of something is, in finance, the adding together of interest or different investments over a period of time such as atoms (1 - the act or process of accruing; 2 - the amount that accrues.) It holds specific meanings in accounting and payroll.

_____, in accounting, describes the accounting method known as _____ basis, whereby revenues and expenses are recognized when they are accrued, i.e. accumulated (earned or incurred), regardless when the actual cash is received or paid out.

a. Earnings before interest, taxes, depreciation and amortization
b. Assets
c. Accrual
d. Accounts receivable

39. _____ is a method of accounting whereby economic activities (rather than cash flow) of financial events are considered, because of two complementary principles, which (together) determine the point, at which expenses and revenues are recognized. According to revenue recognition principle, revenues are realized when earned, whether or not they are received in cash.

a. Accrual
b. Accrual basis accounting
c. Accrued revenue
d. Earnings before interest, taxes, depreciation and amortization

40. In business and accounting, _____ are everything of value that is owned by a person or company. It is a claim on the property your income of a borrower. The balance sheet of a firm records the monetary value of the _____ owned by the firm.

Chapter 1. THE GOVERNMENT AND NOT-FOR-PROFIT ENVIRONMENT

a. Accrual basis accounting

b. Earnings before interest, taxes, depreciation and amortization

c. Accounts receivable

d. Assets

41. In finance, a _____ is a debt security, in which the authorized issuer owes the holders a debt and, depending on the terms of the _____, is obliged to pay interest (the coupon) and/or to repay the principal at a later date, termed maturity. It is a formal contract to repay borrowed money with interest at fixed intervals.

Thus a _____ is like a loan: the issuer is the borrower, the _____ holder is the lender, and the coupon is the interest.

a. Revenue bonds

b. Zero-coupon bond

c. Coupon rate

d. Bond

42. The _____ is a financial market where participants buy and sell debt securities, usually in the form of bonds. As of 2006, the size of the international _____ is an estimated $44.9 trillion, of which the size of the outstanding U.S. _____ debt was $25.2 trillion.

Nearly all of the $923 billion average daily trading volume in the U.S. _____ takes place between broker-dealers and large institutions in a decentralized, over-the-counter market.

a. Convertible bond

b. Demand curve

c. Variance

d. Bond market

43. In economics, _____ or _____ goods or real _____ refers to factors of production used to create goods or services that are not themselves significantly consumed (though they may depreciate) in the production process. _____ goods may be acquired with money or financial _____. In finance and accounting, _____ generally refers to financial wealth, especially that used to start or maintain a business.

a. Vyborg Appeal

b. Disclosure

c. Screening

d. Capital

Chapter 1. THE GOVERNMENT AND NOT-FOR-PROFIT ENVIRONMENT

44. The term _____ has three unrelated technical definitions, and is also used in a variety of non-technical ways.

- In financial economics, it refers to any asset used to make money, as opposed to assets used for personal enjoyment or consumption. This is an important distinction because two people can disagree sharply about the value of personal assets, one person might think a sports car is more valuable than a pickup truck, another person might have the opposite taste. But if an asset is held for the purpose of making money, taste has nothing to do with it, only differences of opinion about how much money the asset will produce. With the further assumption that people agree on the probability distribution of future cash flows, it is possible to have an objective _____ pricing model. Even without the assumption of agreement, it is possible to set rational limits on _____ value.
- In governmental accounting, it is defined as any asset used in operations with an initial useful life extending beyond one reporting period. Generally, government managers have a 'stewardship' duty to maintain _____s under their control. See International Public Sector Accounting Standards for details.
- In US tax accounting, it is defined as any property other than a list of exceptions. The main exceptions are anything held for sale, and any real estate or depreciable property used in business. Almost everything you own and use for personal purposes, pleasure or investment is a _____. If something is a _____ for tax purposes, gains or losses on sale or disposition are capital gains or capital losses. For individuals, however, capital losses on property held for personal use are generally not deductible. See the IRS publication Tax Facts about Capital Gains and Losses for details.

A well-known financial accounting textbook advises that the term be avoided except in tax accounting because it is used in so many different senses, not all of them well-defined. For example it is often used as a synonym for fixed assets or for investments in securities.

A common non-technical usage occurs when people ask that employees or the environment or something else be treated as a _____.

a. BMC Software, Inc.
b. Solvency
c. 3M Company
d. Capital asset

45. A municipality is an administrative entity composed of a clearly defined territory and its population and commonly denotes a city, town or a small grouping of them. A municipality is typically governed by a mayor and a city council or _____ council.

The notion of municipality includes townships but is not restricted to them.

a. Municipal
b. BNSF Railway
c. BMC Software, Inc.
d. 3M Company

46. _____ is a common concept in economics, and gives rise to derived concepts such as consumer debt. Generally _____ is defined by opposition to production. But the precise definition can vary because different schools of economists define production quite differently.
a. Consumption
b. Mitigating Control
c. Yield
d. Starving the beast

Chapter 1. THE GOVERNMENT AND NOT-FOR-PROFIT ENVIRONMENT

47. The _____ duty is a legal relationship of confidence or trust between two or more parties, most commonly a _____ or trustee and a principal or beneficiary. One party, for example a corporate trust company or the trust department of a bank, holds a _____ relation or acts in a _____ capacity to another, such as one whose funds are entrusted to it for investment. In a _____ relation one person justifiably reposes confidence, good faith, reliance and trust in another whose aid, advice or protection is sought in some matter.
   a. FCPA
   b. Robinson-Patman Act
   c. Staple right
   d. Fiduciary

48. _____ is that which is owed; usually referencing assets owed, but the term can also cover moral obligations and other interactions not requiring money. In the case of assets, _____ is a means of using future purchasing power in the present before a summation has been earned. Some companies and corporations use _____ as a part of their overall corporate finance strategy.
   a. Debt
   b. Lender
   c. Loan
   d. Debenture

49. In accounting, _____ has a very specific meaning. It is an outflow of cash or other valuable assets from a person or company to another person or company. This outflow of cash is generally one side of a trade for products or services that have equal or better current or future value to the buyer than to the seller.
   a. ABC Television Network
   b. Expense
   c. AMEX
   d. AIG

50. In financial accounting, a _____ is defined as an obligation of an entity arising from past transactions or events, the settlement of which may result in the transfer or use of assets, provision of services or other yielding of economic benefits in the future.
   a. Corporate governance
   b. Vested
   c. Liability
   d. False Claims Act

51. A _____ is a body of elected or appointed members who jointly oversee the activities of a company or organization. The body sometimes has a different name, such as board of trustees, board of governors, board of managers, or executive board. It is often simply referred to as 'the board.'

A board's activities are determined by the powers, duties, and responsibilities delegated to it or conferred on it by an authority outside itself.

   a. Consumer protection laws
   b. Chief Financial Officers Act of 1990
   c. Hospital Survey and Construction Act
   d. Board of directors

52. The _____ of 2002 (Pub.L. 107-204, 116 Stat. 745, enacted July 30, 2002), also known as the Public Company Accounting Reform and Investor Protection Act of 2002, is a United States federal law enacted on July 30, 2002 in response to a number of major corporate and accounting scandals including those affecting Enron, Tyco International, Adelphia, Peregrine Systems and WorldCom. The legislation establishes new or enhanced standards for all U.S. public company boards, management, and public accounting firms. It does not apply to privately held companies.
   a. Fair Labor Standards Act
   b. Sarbanes-Oxley Act
   c. FCPA
   d. Lease

53. The _____ is located in Norwalk, Connecticut. It is an independent, organization in the private sector that is responsible for oversight of the Financial Accounting Standards Board (FASB), the Governmental Accounting Standards Board (GASB), and their respective advisory councils.

   a. Financial Accounting Foundation
   b. 3M Company
   c. BNSF Railway
   d. BMC Software, Inc.

54. An _____ is a comprehensive report on a company's activities throughout the preceding year. _____s are intended to give shareholders and other interested persons information about the company's activities and financial performance. Most jurisdictions require companies to prepare and disclose _____s, and many require the _____ to be filed at the company's registry.

   a. ABC Television Network
   b. AIG
   c. AMEX
   d. Annual Report

Chapter 2. FUND ACCOUNTING

1. Project _____: The project _____ is a prediction of the costs associated with a particular company project. These costs include labor, materials, and other related expenses. The project _____ is often broken down into specific tasks, with task _____s assigned to each.
   a. BMC Software, Inc.
   b. 3M Company
   c. Budget
   d. BNSF Railway

2. The _____ is a federal agency within the legislative branch of the United States government. It is a government agency that provides economic data to Congress. It was created by the Congressional Budget and Impoundment Control Act of 1974.
   a. 3M Company
   b. Congressional Budget Office
   c. General Accounting Office
   d. BMC Software, Inc.

3. The _____ is currently the source of generally accepted accounting principles (GAAP) used by State and Local governments in the [[United States of America]]. As with most of the entities involved in creating GAAP in the United States, it is a private, non-governmental organization.

   The _____ is subject to oversight by the Financial Accounting Foundation (FAF), which selects the members of the _____ and the Financial Accounting Standards Board, and funds both organizations.

   a. Multinational corporation
   b. Fannie Mae
   c. National Conference of Commissioners on Uniform State Laws
   d. Governmental Accounting Standards Board

4. The _____ is a Cabinet-level office, and is the largest office within the Executive Office of the President of the United States (EOP.) It is an important conduit by which the White House oversees the activities of federal agencies. OMB is tasked with giving expert advice to senior White House officials on a range of topics relating to federal policy, management, legislative, regulatory, and budgetary issues.
   a. Alaska Air Group
   b. AT'T Wireless Services, Inc.
   c. Analysis of variance
   d. Office of Management and Budget

5. _____ is an accounting system often used by nonprofit organizations and by the public sector. According to StartHereGoPlaces, _____ is a '[m]ethod of accounting and presentation whereby assets and liabilities are grouped according to the purpose for which they are to be used.'

   _____ serves any nonprofit organization or the public sector. These organizations have a need for special reporting to financial statements users that show how money is spent, rather than how much profit was earned.

   a. Refunding
   b. Replacement cost
   c. Fund accounting
   d. Liquidating dividend

6. _____ is the term used to refer to the standard framework of guidelines for financial accounting used in any given jurisdiction. _____ includes the standards, conventions, and rules accountants follow in recording and summarizing transactions, and in the preparation of financial statements.

   Financial accounting information must be assembled and reported objectively.

a. Current asset
b. General ledger
c. Long-term liabilities
d. Generally accepted accounting principles

7. The _____ was established as the _____ by the Budget and Accounting Act of 1921 (Pub.L. 67-13, 42 Stat. 20, June 10, 1921.)
a. 3M Company
b. BMC Software, Inc.
c. GAO
d. General Accounting Office

8. The _____ is the national, professional association of CPAs in the United States, with more than 330,000 members, including CPAs in business and industry, public practice, government, and education; student affiliates; and international associates. It sets ethical standards for the profession and U.S. auditing standards for audits of private companies; federal, state and local governments; and non-profit organizations.

Approximately 40% of its members are engaged in the practice of public accounting, in areas such as auditing, accounting, taxation, general business consulting, business valuation, personal financial planning and business technology.

a. ABC Television Network
b. AIG
c. Other postemployment benefits
d. American Institute of Certified Public Accountants

9. The _____ is a private, not-for-profit organization whose primary purpose is to develop generally accepted accounting principles (GAAP) within the United States in the public's interest. The Securities and Exchange Commission (SEC) designated the _____ as the organization responsible for setting accounting standards for public companies in the U.S. It was created in 1973, replacing the Accounting Principles Board and the Committee on Accounting Procedure of the American Institute of Certified Public Accountants. The _____'s mission is 'to establish and improve standards of financial accounting and reporting for the guidance and education of the public, including issuers, auditors, and users of financial information.'

The _____ is not a governmental body.

a. Governmental Accounting Standards Board
b. Fannie Mae
c. Public company
d. Financial Accounting Standards Board

10. _____ are formal records of a business' financial activities.

In British English, including United Kingdom company law, _____ are often referred to as accounts, although the term _____ is also used, particularly by accountants.

_____ provide an overview of a business' financial condition in both short and long term.

a. Statement of retained earnings
b. 3M Company
c. Notes to the financial statements
d. Financial statements

Chapter 2. FUND ACCOUNTING

11. The _____ after Senator Harold Burton of Ohio and Senator Lister Hill of Alabama, is a United States federal law passed in 1946. This act responded to the first of Trumane;s proposals and was designed to provide federal grants and guaranteed loans to improve the physical plant of the natione;s hospital system. Money was designated to the states to achieve 4.5 beds per 1,000 people.

   a. Tax patent
   b. Model Code of Professional Responsibility
   c. Lease
   d. Hospital Survey and Construction Act

12. A _____ is a fungible, negotiable instrument representing financial value. they are broadly categorized into debt securities (such as banknotes, bonds and debentures), and equity securities; e.g., common stocks. The company or other entity issuing the _____ is called the issuer.

   a. 3M Company
   b. BMC Software, Inc.
   c. Tracking stock
   d. Security

13. _____ in the United States currently refers to the federal Old-Age, Survivors, and Disability Insurance (OASDI) program.

The original _____ Act and the current version of the Act, as amended encompass several social welfare and social insurance programs. The larger and better known programs are:

- Federal Old-Age, Survivors, and Disability Insurance
- Unemployment benefits
- Temporary Assistance for Needy Families
- Health Insurance for Aged and Disabled (Medicare)
- Grants to States for Medical Assistance Programs (Medicaid)
- State Children's Health Insurance Program (SCHIP)
- Supplemental Security Income (Social SecurityI)

U.S. _____ is a social insurance program funded through dedicated payroll taxes called Federal Insurance Contributions Act (FICA.) Tax deposits are formally entrusted to Federal Old-Age and Survivors Insurance Trust Fund, or Federal Disability Insurance Trust Fund, Federal Hospital Insurance Trust Fund or the Federal Supplementary Medical Insurance Trust Fund.

   a. Sale
   b. Social Security
   c. Comparable
   d. Price-to-sales ratio

14. The United States _____ is an independent agency of the United States federal government that administers Social Security, a social insurance program consisting of retirement, disability, and survivors' benefits. To qualify for these benefits, most American workers pay Social Security taxes on their earnings; future benefits are based on the employees' contributions.

The _____ was established by a law currently codified at 42 U.S.C.

   a. Minority interest
   b. Social Security Administration
   c. Return on assets
   d. Time value of money

Chapter 2. FUND ACCOUNTING

15. To tax is to impose a financial charge or other levy upon a _____ by a state or the functional equivalent of a state.

Taxes are also imposed by many subnational entities. Taxes consist of direct tax or indirect tax, and may be paid in money or as its labour equivalent (often but not always unpaid.)

    a. Taxpayer
    c. Federal Unemployment Tax Act
    b. Tax avoidance
    d. State tax levels

16. In accounting, _____ has a very specific meaning. It is an outflow of cash or other valuable assets from a person or company to another person or company. This outflow of cash is generally one side of a trade for products or services that have equal or better current or future value to the buyer than to the seller.

    a. AIG
    c. AMEX
    b. ABC Television Network
    d. Expense

Chapter 3. ISSUES OF BUDGETING AND CONTROL   17

1. The _____ is currently the source of generally accepted accounting principles (GAAP) used by State and Local governments in the [[United States of America]]. As with most of the entities involved in creating GAAP in the United States, it is a private, non-governmental organization.

The _____ is subject to oversight by the Financial Accounting Foundation (FAF), which selects the members of the _____ and the Financial Accounting Standards Board, and funds both organizations.

- a. Fannie Mae
- b. Governmental Accounting Standards Board
- c. National Conference of Commissioners on Uniform State Laws
- d. Multinational corporation

2. Project _____: The project _____ is a prediction of the costs associated with a particular company project. These costs include labor, materials, and other related expenses. The project _____ is often broken down into specific tasks, with task _____s assigned to each.
- a. 3M Company
- b. Budget
- c. BNSF Railway
- d. BMC Software, Inc.

3. The _____ is a federal agency within the legislative branch of the United States government. It is a government agency that provides economic data to Congress. It was created by the Congressional Budget and Impoundment Control Act of 1974.
- a. Congressional Budget Office
- b. BMC Software, Inc.
- c. General Accounting Office
- d. 3M Company

4. _____ is the act of taking possession of or assigning purpose to properties or ideas and is important in many topics, including:

- _____ in relation to the spread of knowledge
- _____ (art)
  - _____ (music) in reference to the re-use and proliferation of different types of music
- _____ (economics) origination of human ownership of previously unowned natural resources such as land
- _____ (law) as a component of government spending
- Cultural _____ is the borrowing, or theft, of an element of cultural expression of one group by another.
- The tort of _____ is one form of invasion of privacy.

- a. Intangible
- b. Improvement
- c. Annuity
- d. Appropriation

5. In business and accounting, _____ are everything of value that is owned by a person or company. It is a claim on the property your income of a borrower. The balance sheet of a firm records the monetary value of the _____ owned by the firm.
- a. Accrual basis accounting
- b. Accounts receivable
- c. Assets
- d. Earnings before interest, taxes, depreciation and amortization

6. In economics, _____ or _____ goods or real _____ refers to factors of production used to create goods or services that are not themselves significantly consumed (though they may depreciate) in the production process. _____ goods may be acquired with money or financial _____. In finance and accounting, _____ generally refers to financial wealth, especially that used to start or maintain a business.

   a. Screening
   b. Vyborg Appeal
   c. Capital
   d. Disclosure

7. The term _____ has three unrelated technical definitions, and is also used in a variety of non-technical ways.

   - In financial economics, it refers to any asset used to make money, as opposed to assets used for personal enjoyment or consumption. This is an important distinction because two people can disagree sharply about the value of personal assets, one person might think a sports car is more valuable than a pickup truck, another person might have the opposite taste. But if an asset is held for the purpose of making money, taste has nothing to do with it, only differences of opinion about how much money the asset will produce. With the further assumption that people agree on the probability distribution of future cash flows, it is possible to have an objective _____ pricing model. Even without the assumption of agreement, it is possible to set rational limits on _____ value.
   - In governmental accounting, it is defined as any asset used in operations with an initial useful life extending beyond one reporting period. Generally, government managers have a 'stewardship' duty to maintain _____s under their control. See International Public Sector Accounting Standards for details.
   - In US tax accounting, it is defined as any property other than a list of exceptions. The main exceptions are anything held for sale, and any real estate or depreciable property used in business. Almost everything you own and use for personal purposes, pleasure or investment is a _____. If something is a _____ for tax purposes, gains or losses on sale or disposition are capital gains or capital losses. For individuals, however, capital losses on property held for personal use are generally not deductible. See the IRS publication Tax Facts about Capital Gains and Losses for details.

A well-known financial accounting textbook advises that the term be avoided except in tax accounting because it is used in so many different senses, not all of them well-defined. For example it is often used as a synonym for fixed assets or for investments in securities.

A common non-technical usage occurs when people ask that employees or the environment or something else be treated as a _____.

   a. Solvency
   b. 3M Company
   c. BMC Software, Inc.
   d. Capital asset

8. _____ is the planning process used to determine whether a firm's long term investments such as new machinery, replacement machinery, new plants, new products, and research development projects are worth pursuing. It is budget for major capital, or investment, expenditures.

Chapter 3. ISSUES OF BUDGETING AND CONTROL

Many formal methods are used in _____, including the techniques such as

- Net present value
- Profitability index
- Internal rate of return
- Modified Internal Rate of Return
- Equivalent annuity

These methods use the incremental cash flows from each potential investment, or project. Techniques based on accounting earnings and accounting rules are sometimes used - though economists consider this to be improper - such as the accounting rate of return, and 'return on investment.' Simplified and hybrid methods are used as well, such as payback period and discounted payback period.

a. Preferred stock
c. Cash flow
b. Gross profit
d. Capital budgeting

9. _____ is the process of estimation in unknown situations. Prediction is a similar, but more general term. Both can refer to estimation of time series, cross-sectional or longitudinal data.
   a. Forecasting
   b. BMC Software, Inc.
   c. 3M Company
   d. BNSF Railway

10. _____ are sometimes the same as net worth, or shareholders' equity - assets minus liabilities. The term _____ is commonly used with charities or not for profit entities. Although these entities don't make money, it is important to maintain reasonable reserves to help future growth.
    a. Net interest spread
    b. Sortino ratio
    c. Net assets
    d. Debtor days

11. An _____ is the annual budget of an activity stated in terms of Budget Classification Code, functional/subfunctional categories and cost accounts. It contains estimates of the total value of resources required for the performance of the operation including reimbursable work or services for others. It also includes estimates of workload in terms of total work units identified by cost accounts.
    a. Inventory turnover ratio
    b. Authorised capital
    c. Internality
    d. Operating budget

12. The _____ is the national, professional association of CPAs in the United States, with more than 330,000 members, including CPAs in business and industry, public practice, government, and education; student affiliates; and international associates. It sets ethical standards for the profession and U.S. auditing standards for audits of private companies; federal, state and local governments; and non-profit organizations.

Approximately 40% of its members are engaged in the practice of public accounting, in areas such as auditing, accounting, taxation, general business consulting, business valuation, personal financial planning and business technology.

a. AIG
b. American Institute of Certified Public Accountants
c. Other postemployment benefits
d. ABC Television Network

13. The _____ is a private, not-for-profit organization whose primary purpose is to develop generally accepted accounting principles (GAAP) within the United States in the public's interest. The Securities and Exchange Commission (SEC) designated the _____ as the organization responsible for setting accounting standards for public companies in the U.S. It was created in 1973, replacing the Accounting Principles Board and the Committee on Accounting Procedure of the American Institute of Certified Public Accountants. The _____'s mission is 'to establish and improve standards of financial accounting and reporting for the guidance and education of the public, including issuers, auditors, and users of financial information.'

The _____ is not a governmental body.

a. Public company
b. Fannie Mae
c. Governmental Accounting Standards Board
d. Financial Accounting Standards Board

14. _____, also known as property, plant, and equipment (PP&E), is a term used in accountancy for assets and property which cannot easily be converted into cash. This can be compared with current assets such as cash or bank accounts, which are described as liquid assets. In most cases, only tangible assets are referred to as fixed.

a. Bankruptcy prediction
b. Fixed asset
c. Subledger
d. Minority interest

15. _____ is an accounting system often used by nonprofit organizations and by the public sector. According to StartHereGoPlaces, _____ is a '[m]ethod of accounting and presentation whereby assets and liabilities are grouped according to the purpose for which they are to be used.'

_____ serves any nonprofit organization or the public sector. These organizations have a need for special reporting to financial statements users that show how money is spent, rather than how much profit was earned.

a. Replacement cost
b. Liquidating dividend
c. Refunding
d. Fund accounting

16. The term _____ usually refers to a company that is permitted to offer its registered securities (stock, bonds, etc.) for sale to the general public, typically through a stock exchange, or occasionally a company whose stock is traded over the counter (OTC) via market makers who use non-exchange quotation services.

The term '_____' may also refer to a company owned by the government.

a. Governmental Accounting Standards Board
b. Professional association
c. MicroStrategy
d. Public Company

Chapter 3. ISSUES OF BUDGETING AND CONTROL

17. The _____ (sometimes called 'Peekaboo') is a private-sector, non-profit corporation created by the Sarbanes-Oxley Act, a 2002 United States federal law, to oversee the auditors of public companies. Its stated purpose is to 'protect the interests of investors and further the public interest in the preparation of informative, fair, and independent audit reports'. Although a private entity, the _____ has many government-like regulatory functions, making it in some ways similar to the private Self Regulatory Organizations (SROs) that regulate stock markets and other aspects of the financial markets in the United States.
   a. Pension Benefit Guaranty Corporation
   b. Public Company Accounting Oversight Board
   c. Financial Crimes Enforcement Network
   d. 3M Company

18. A _____ refers to the process by which governments create and approve a budget. Â· The Financial Service Department prepares worksheets to assist the department head in preparation of department budget estimates Â· The Administrator calls a meeting of managers and they present and discuss plans for the following yeare;s projected level of activity. Â· The managers can work with the Financial Services, or work alone to prepare an estimate for the departments coming year.
   a. BMC Software, Inc.
   b. 3M Company
   c. BNSF Railway
   d. Budget process

19. The _____ after Senator Harold Burton of Ohio and Senator Lister Hill of Alabama, is a United States federal law passed in 1946. This act responded to the first of Trumane;s proposals and was designed to provide federal grants and guaranteed loans to improve the physical plant of the natione;s hospital system. Money was designated to the states to achieve 4.5 beds per 1,000 people.
   a. Tax patent
   b. Model Code of Professional Responsibility
   c. Lease
   d. Hospital Survey and Construction Act

20. The _____ is a Cabinet-level office, and is the largest office within the Executive Office of the President of the United States (EOP.) It is an important conduit by which the White House oversees the activities of federal agencies. OMB is tasked with giving expert advice to senior White House officials on a range of topics relating to federal policy, management, legislative, regulatory, and budgetary issues.
   a. Alaska Air Group
   b. Analysis of variance
   c. AT'T Wireless Services, Inc.
   d. Office of Management and Budget

21. _____ is the term used to refer to the standard framework of guidelines for financial accounting used in any given jurisdiction. _____ includes the standards, conventions, and rules accountants follow in recording and summarizing transactions, and in the preparation of financial statements.

Financial accounting information must be assembled and reported objectively.

   a. Long-term liabilities
   b. Generally accepted accounting principles
   c. Current asset
   d. General ledger

22. The _____ was established as the _____ by the Budget and Accounting Act of 1921 (Pub.L. 67-13, 42 Stat. 20, June 10, 1921.)
   a. BMC Software, Inc.
   b. General Accounting Office
   c. GAO
   d. 3M Company

Chapter 3. ISSUES OF BUDGETING AND CONTROL

23. _____ is an umbrella term which refers to the various accounting systems used by various public sector entities. In the United States, for instance, there are two levels of government which follow different accounting standards set forth by independent, private sector boards. At the federal level, the Federal Accounting Standards Advisory Board (FASAB) sets forth the accounting standards to follow.
   a. Product control
   b. Management accounting
   c. Nonassurance services
   d. Governmental Accounting

24. _____ of something is, in finance, the adding together of interest or different investments over a period of time such as atoms (1 - the act or process of accruing; 2 - the amount that accrues.) It holds specific meanings in accounting and payroll.

   _____, in accounting, describes the accounting method known as _____ basis, whereby revenues and expenses are recognized when they are accrued, i.e. accumulated (earned or incurred), regardless when the actual cash is received or paid out.
   a. Assets
   b. Accounts receivable
   c. Accrual
   d. Earnings before interest, taxes, depreciation and amortization

25. _____ is a method of accounting whereby economic activities (rather than cash flow) of financial events are considered, because of two complementary principles, which (together) determine the point, at which expenses and revenues are recognized. According to revenue recognition principle, revenues are realized when earned, whether or not they are received in cash.
   a. Earnings before interest, taxes, depreciation and amortization
   b. Accrual
   c. Accrued revenue
   d. Accrual basis accounting

26. An _____ is a comprehensive report on a company's activities throughout the preceding year. _____s are intended to give shareholders and other interested persons information about the company's activities and financial performance. Most jurisdictions require companies to prepare and disclose _____s, and many require the _____ to be filed at the company's registry.
   a. ABC Television Network
   b. AMEX
   c. AIG
   d. Annual report

27. _____ is a legal term of art for anything that affects or limits the title of a property, such as mortgages, leases, easements, liens, or restrictions. Also, those considered as potentially making the title defeasible are also _____s. For example, charging orders, building orders and structure alteration.
   a. Ownership
   b. Administrative proceeding
   c. ABC Television Network
   d. Encumbrance

28. _____ is concerned with the provisions and use of accounting information to managers within organizations, to provide them with the basis to make informed business decisions that will allow them to be better equipped in their management and control functions.

Chapter 3. ISSUES OF BUDGETING AND CONTROL

In contrast to financial accountancy information, _____ information is:

- usually confidential and used by management, instead of publicly reported;
- forward-looking, instead of historical;
- pragmatically computed using extensive management information systems and internal controls, instead of complying with accounting standards.

This is because of the different emphasis: _____ information is used within an organization, typically for decision-making.

a. Nonassurance services
b. Grenzplankostenrechnung
c. Governmental accounting
d. Management accounting

29. The _____ of a company or public agency is the corporate officer primarily responsible for managing the financial risks of the business or agency. This officer is also responsible for financial planning and record-keeping, as well as financial reporting to higher management. (In recent years, however, the role has expanded to encompass communicating financial performance and forecasts to the analyst community.)

a. Chief executive officer
b. Merck ' Co., Inc.
c. Chief Financial Officer
d. NASDAQ

30. The _____ signed into law by President George H.W. Bush on November 15, 1990, is a United States federal law intended to improve the government's financial management, outlining standards of financial performance and disclosure. Among other measures, the Office of Management and Budget (OMB) was given greater authority over federal financial management. For each of 23 federal departments and agencies, the position of chief financial officer was created.

a. Jenkins Committee
b. Scottish Poor Laws
c. Bylaw
d. Chief Financial Officers Act of 1990

31. A _____ has several related meanings:

- a daily record of events or business; a private _____ is usually referred to as a diary.
- a newspaper or other periodical, in the literal sense of one published each day;
- many publications issued at stated intervals, such as magazines, or scholarly academic _____s, or the record of the transactions of a society, are often called _____s. Although _____ is sometimes used, erroneously, as a synonym for 'magazine,' in academic use, a _____ refers to a serious, scholarly publication, most often peer-reviewed. A non-scholarly magazine written for an educated audience about an industry or an area of professional activity is usually called a professional magazine.

The word 'journalist' for one whose business is writing for the public press has been in use since the end of the 17th century.

Open access _____s are scholarly _____s that are available to the reader without financial or other barrier other than access to the internet itself. Some are subsidized, and some require payment on behalf of the author. Subsidized _____s are financed by an academic institution or a government information center.

a. 3M Company
c. BNSF Railway
b. Journal
d. BMC Software, Inc.

32. _____ and credit are formal bookkeeping and accounting terms. They are the most fundamental concepts in accounting, representing the two records that one party in a transaction makes on its records, transferring a money balance from one account to another, one representing a reduction of liability or increase in asset, and the other representing a balancing increase in liability or reduction of asset.

Introduction

_____s and credits are a system of notation used in accounting to keep track of money movements (transactions) into and out of an account.

a. Debit and credit
c. Debit
b. Bookkeeping
d. Cookie jar accounting

33. An _____ is a term used in behavioral economics to describe those types of behaviors that impose costs on a person in the long-run that are not taken into account when making decisions in the present. Classical Economics discourages government from creating legislation that targets internalities, because it is assumed that the consumer takes these personal costs into account when paying for the good that causes the _____. For example, cigarettes should be taxed because of the negative consumption externalities that they impose, such as second-hand smoke, not because the smoker harms him or herself by smoking.
a. Authorised capital
c. Operating budget
b. Inventory turnover ratio
d. Internality

34. The word _____ indicates that a party, or proprietor, exercises private ownership, control or use over an item of property
a. Proprietary
c. BMC Software, Inc.
b. BNSF Railway
d. 3M Company

Chapter 4. RECOGNIZING REVENUES IN GOVERNMENTAL FUNDS

1. The _____ is the national, professional association of CPAs in the United States, with more than 330,000 members, including CPAs in business and industry, public practice, government, and education; student affiliates; and international associates. It sets ethical standards for the profession and U.S. auditing standards for audits of private companies; federal, state and local governments; and non-profit organizations.

Approximately 40% of its members are engaged in the practice of public accounting, in areas such as auditing, accounting, taxation, general business consulting, business valuation, personal financial planning and business technology.

   a. Other postemployment benefits
   b. ABC Television Network
   c. AIG
   d. American Institute of Certified Public Accountants

2. Project _____: The project _____ is a prediction of the costs associated with a particular company project. These costs include labor, materials, and other related expenses. The project _____ is often broken down into specific tasks, with task _____s assigned to each.
   a. BMC Software, Inc.
   b. 3M Company
   c. BNSF Railway
   d. Budget

3. The _____ is a federal agency within the legislative branch of the United States government. It is a government agency that provides economic data to Congress. It was created by the Congressional Budget and Impoundment Control Act of 1974.
   a. 3M Company
   b. General Accounting Office
   c. BMC Software, Inc.
   d. Congressional Budget Office

4. The _____ is a private, not-for-profit organization whose primary purpose is to develop generally accepted accounting principles (GAAP) within the United States in the public's interest. The Securities and Exchange Commission (SEC) designated the _____ as the organization responsible for setting accounting standards for public companies in the U.S. It was created in 1973, replacing the Accounting Principles Board and the Committee on Accounting Procedure of the American Institute of Certified Public Accountants. The _____'s mission is 'to establish and improve standards of financial accounting and reporting for the guidance and education of the public, including issuers, auditors, and users of financial information.'

The _____ is not a governmental body.

   a. Governmental Accounting Standards Board
   b. Public company
   c. Fannie Mae
   d. Financial Accounting Standards Board

5. _____ is the term used to refer to the standard framework of guidelines for financial accounting used in any given jurisdiction. _____ includes the standards, conventions, and rules accountants follow in recording and summarizing transactions, and in the preparation of financial statements.

Financial accounting information must be assembled and reported objectively.

   a. Current asset
   b. General ledger
   c. Long-term liabilities
   d. Generally accepted accounting principles

Chapter 4. RECOGNIZING REVENUES IN GOVERNMENTAL FUNDS

6. The _____ was established as the _____ by the Budget and Accounting Act of 1921 (Pub.L. 67-13, 42 Stat. 20, June 10, 1921.)
   a. General Accounting Office
   b. GAO
   c. 3M Company
   d. BMC Software, Inc.

7. The _____ is currently the source of generally accepted accounting principles (GAAP) used by State and Local governments in the [[United States of America]]. As with most of the entities involved in creating GAAP in the United States, it is a private, non-governmental organization.

The _____ is subject to oversight by the Financial Accounting Foundation (FAF), which selects the members of the _____ and the Financial Accounting Standards Board, and funds both organizations.

   a. Multinational corporation
   b. Fannie Mae
   c. National Conference of Commissioners on Uniform State Laws
   d. Governmental Accounting Standards Board

8. A _____ is a fungible, negotiable instrument representing financial value. they are broadly categorized into debt securities (such as banknotes, bonds and debentures), and equity securities; e.g., common stocks. The company or other entity issuing the _____ is called the issuer.
   a. Security
   b. BMC Software, Inc.
   c. 3M Company
   d. Tracking stock

9. _____ in the United States currently refers to the federal Old-Age, Survivors, and Disability Insurance (OASDI) program.

The original _____ Act and the current version of the Act, as amended encompass several social welfare and social insurance programs. The larger and better known programs are:

- Federal Old-Age, Survivors, and Disability Insurance
- Unemployment benefits
- Temporary Assistance for Needy Families
- Health Insurance for Aged and Disabled (Medicare)
- Grants to States for Medical Assistance Programs (Medicaid)
- State Children's Health Insurance Program (SCHIP)
- Supplemental Security Income (Social Securityl)

U.S. _____ is a social insurance program funded through dedicated payroll taxes called Federal Insurance Contributions Act (FICA.) Tax deposits are formally entrusted to Federal Old-Age and Survivors Insurance Trust Fund, or Federal Disability Insurance Trust Fund, Federal Hospital Insurance Trust Fund or the Federal Supplementary Medical Insurance Trust Fund.

   a. Social Security
   b. Sale
   c. Price-to-sales ratio
   d. Comparable

Chapter 4. RECOGNIZING REVENUES IN GOVERNMENTAL FUNDS 27

10. The United States _____ is an independent agency of the United States federal government that administers Social Security, a social insurance program consisting of retirement, disability, and survivors' benefits. To qualify for these benefits, most American workers pay Social Security taxes on their earnings; future benefits are based on the employees' contributions.

The _____ was established by a law currently codified at 42 U.S.C.

  a. Minority interest
  b. Return on assets
  c. Social Security Administration
  d. Time value of money

11. An _____ is a comprehensive report on a company's activities throughout the preceding year. _____s are intended to give shareholders and other interested persons information about the company's activities and financial performance. Most jurisdictions require companies to prepare and disclose _____s, and many require the _____ to be filed at the company's registry.
  a. ABC Television Network
  b. AMEX
  c. AIG
  d. Annual report

12. _____ are formal records of a business' financial activities.

In British English, including United Kingdom company law, _____ are often referred to as accounts, although the term _____ is also used, particularly by accountants.

_____ provide an overview of a business' financial condition in both short and long term.

  a. Statement of retained earnings
  b. Notes to the financial statements
  c. 3M Company
  d. Financial statements

13. _____ are annual financial statements or reports for the year. The financial statements, in contrast to budget, present the revenue collected and amounts spent. The _____ usually include a statement of activities (similar to an income statement in the private sector), a balance sheet and often some type of reconciliation.
  a. Government financial statements
  b. BNSF Railway
  c. 3M Company
  d. BMC Software, Inc.

14. _____ is any physical or virtual entity that is owned by an individual or jointly by a group of individuals. An owner of _____ has the right to consume, sell, rent, mortgage, transfer and exchange his or her _____. Important widely-recognized types of _____ include real _____, personal _____ (other physical possessions), and intellectual _____ (rights over artistic creations, inventions, etc.), although the latter is not always as widely recognized or enforced.
  a. Primary authority
  b. Disclosure requirement
  c. Fiduciary
  d. Property

15. _____ principle is a cornerstone of accrual accounting together with matching principle. They both determine the accounting period, in which revenues and expenses are recognized. According to the principle, revenues are recognized when they are (1) realized or realizable, and are (2) earned (usually when goods are transferred or services rendered), no matter when cash is received.

a. Net realizable value
b. BMC Software, Inc.
c. Revenue recognition
d. 3M Company

16. An _____ is a tax based on the value of real estate or personal property. It is more common than the opposite, a specific duty, or a tax based on the quantity of an item regardless of price.

An _____ is typically imposed at the time of a transaction), but it may be imposed on an annual basis (real or personal property tax) or in connection with another significant event (inheritance tax, surrendering citizenship, or tariffs.)

a. Optimal tax
b. Entertainment tax
c. User charge
d. Ad valorem tax

17. A maritime _____ is a _____ on a vessel, given to secure the claim of a creditor who provided maritime services to the vessel or who suffered an injury from the vessel's use. Maritime _____s are sometimes referred to as tacit hypothecation. Maritime _____s have little in common with other _____s under the laws of most jurisdictions.
a. Lien
b. Vested
c. Recharacterisation
d. Fiduciary

18. A _____ is any one of a variety of different systems, institutions, procedures, social relations and infrastructures whereby persons trade, and goods and services are exchanged, forming part of the economy. It is an arrangement that allows buyers and sellers to exchange things. _____s vary in size, range, geographic scale, location, types and variety of human communities, as well as the types of goods and services traded.
a. Perfect competition
b. Recession
c. Market Failure
d. Market

19. _____ is the price at which an asset would trade in a competitive Walrasian auction setting. _____ is often used interchangeably with open _____, fair value or fair _____, although these terms have distinct definitions in different standards, and may differ in some circumstances.

International Valuation Standards defines _____ as 'the estimated amount for which a property should exchange on the date of valuation between a willing buyer and a willing seller in an arme;s-length transaction after proper marketing wherein the parties had each acted knowledgeably, prudently, and without compulsion.'

_____ is a concept distinct from market price, which is e;the price at which one can transacte;, while _____ is e;the true underlying valuee; according to theoretical standards.

a. Sinking fund
b. Segregated portfolio company
c. Debtor
d. Market value

20. The term _____ usually refers to a company that is permitted to offer its registered securities (stock, bonds, etc.) for sale to the general public, typically through a stock exchange, or occasionally a company whose stock is traded over the counter (OTC) via market makers who use non-exchange quotation services.

The term '_____' may also refer to a company owned by the government.

Chapter 4. RECOGNIZING REVENUES IN GOVERNMENTAL FUNDS

a. Governmental Accounting Standards Board
b. MicroStrategy
c. Professional association
d. Public Company

21. The _____ (sometimes called 'Peekaboo') is a private-sector, non-profit corporation created by the Sarbanes-Oxley Act, a 2002 United States federal law, to oversee the auditors of public companies. Its stated purpose is to 'protect the interests of investors and further the public interest in the preparation of informative, fair, and independent audit reports'. Although a private entity, the _____ has many government-like regulatory functions, making it in some ways similar to the private Self Regulatory Organizations (SROs) that regulate stock markets and other aspects of the financial markets in the United States.

a. Public Company Accounting Oversight Board
b. Pension Benefit Guaranty Corporation
c. 3M Company
d. Financial Crimes Enforcement Network

22. A _____ is the pinnacle activity involved in selling products or services in return for money or other compensation. It is an act of completion of a commercial activity.

A _____ is completed by the seller, the owner of the goods.

a. Sale
b. High yield stock
c. Maturity
d. Tertiary sector of economy

23. _____ are the income that is gained by governments because of taxation of the people.

Just as there are different types of tax, the form in which _____ is collected also differs; furthermore, the agency that collects the tax may not be part of central government, but may be an alternative third-party licenced to collect tax which they themselves will use. For example:

- In the UK, the DVLA collects road tax, which is then passed on the treasury.

_____s on purchases can come from two forms: 'tax' itself is a percentage of the price added to the purchase (such as sales tax in US states, or VAT in the UK), while 'duty' is a fixed amount added to the purchase price (such as is commonly found on cigarettes.) In order to calculate the total tax raised from these sales, we must work out the effective tax rate multiplied by the quantity supplied.

a. Tax revenue
b. Life insurance tax shelter
c. National War Tax Resistance Coordinating Committee
d. Disposable income

24. The _____ after Senator Harold Burton of Ohio and Senator Lister Hill of Alabama, is a United States federal law passed in 1946. This act responded to the first of Trumane;s proposals and was designed to provide federal grants and guaranteed loans to improve the physical plant of the natione;s hospital system. Money was designated to the states to achieve 4.5 beds per 1,000 people.

a. Lease
b. Tax patent
c. Model Code of Professional Responsibility
d. Hospital Survey and Construction Act

Chapter 4. RECOGNIZING REVENUES IN GOVERNMENTAL FUNDS

25. _____ is a tax charged by some US states to corporations formed in those states based on the number of shares they issue or, in some cases, the amount of their assets. The purpose of the tax is to raise revenue for the state. The State of Delaware has a significant _____, while other states, such as Nevada, have none at all or a smaller one.
    a. Special-purpose local-option sales tax
    b. Franchise tax
    c. Tax shift
    d. Partnership taxation

26. An _____ is a tax levied on the financial income of people, corporations, or other legal entities. Various _____ systems exist, with varying degrees of tax incidence. Income taxation can be progressive, proportional, or regressive.
    a. Ordinary income
    b. Implied level of government service
    c. Individual Retirement Arrangement
    d. Income tax

27. A _____ is the transfer of wealth from one party (such as a person or company) to another. A _____ is usually made in exchange for the provision of goods, services or both, or to fulfill a legal obligation.

    The simplest and oldest form of _____ is barter, the exchange of one good or service for another.

    a. Payee
    b. BMC Software, Inc.
    c. 3M Company
    d. Payment

28. The word _____ indicates that a party, or proprietor, exercises private ownership, control or use over an item of property
    a. Proprietary
    b. 3M Company
    c. BMC Software, Inc.
    d. BNSF Railway

29. In business and accounting, _____ are everything of value that is owned by a person or company. It is a claim on the property your income of a borrower. The balance sheet of a firm records the monetary value of the _____ owned by the firm.
    a. Earnings before interest, taxes, depreciation and amortization
    b. Accrual basis accounting
    c. Accounts receivable
    d. Assets

30. In economics, _____ or _____ goods or real _____ refers to factors of production used to create goods or services that are not themselves significantly consumed (though they may depreciate) in the production process. _____ goods may be acquired with money or financial _____. In finance and accounting, _____ generally refers to financial wealth, especially that used to start or maintain a business.
    a. Vyborg Appeal
    b. Capital
    c. Screening
    d. Disclosure

Chapter 4. RECOGNIZING REVENUES IN GOVERNMENTAL FUNDS

31. The term _____ has three unrelated technical definitions, and is also used in a variety of non-technical ways.

    - In financial economics, it refers to any asset used to make money, as opposed to assets used for personal enjoyment or consumption. This is an important distinction because two people can disagree sharply about the value of personal assets, one person might think a sports car is more valuable than a pickup truck, another person might have the opposite taste. But if an asset is held for the purpose of making money, taste has nothing to do with it, only differences of opinion about how much money the asset will produce. With the further assumption that people agree on the probability distribution of future cash flows, it is possible to have an objective _____ pricing model. Even without the assumption of agreement, it is possible to set rational limits on _____ value.
    - In governmental accounting, it is defined as any asset used in operations with an initial useful life extending beyond one reporting period. Generally, government managers have a 'stewardship' duty to maintain _____s under their control. See International Public Sector Accounting Standards for details.
    - In US tax accounting, it is defined as any property other than a list of exceptions. The main exceptions are anything held for sale, and any real estate or depreciable property used in business. Almost everything you own and use for personal purposes, pleasure or investment is a _____. If something is a _____ for tax purposes, gains or losses on sale or disposition are capital gains or capital losses. For individuals, however, capital losses on property held for personal use are generally not deductible. See the IRS publication Tax Facts about Capital Gains and Losses for details.

    A well-known financial accounting textbook advises that the term be avoided except in tax accounting because it is used in so many different senses, not all of them well-defined. For example it is often used as a synonym for fixed assets or for investments in securities.

    A common non-technical usage occurs when people ask that employees or the environment or something else be treated as a _____.

    a. Solvency
    b. 3M Company
    c. BMC Software, Inc.
    d. Capital asset

32. The _____ is a Cabinet-level office, and is the largest office within the Executive Office of the President of the United States (EOP.) It is an important conduit by which the White House oversees the activities of federal agencies. OMB is tasked with giving expert advice to senior White House officials on a range of topics relating to federal policy, management, legislative, regulatory, and budgetary issues.
    a. Office of Management and Budget
    b. Alaska Air Group
    c. Analysis of variance
    d. AT'T Wireless Services, Inc.

33. The US _____, historically and commonly known as the Food Stamp Program, is a federal assistance program that provides food to low and no income people living in the United States. Benefits are distributed by the individual states, but the program is administered through the U.S. Department of Agriculture. Most food stamp benefits are now distributed using cards but for most of its history the program had actually used paper denominational stamps/coupons worth $1, $5, and $10.
    a. BMC Software, Inc.
    b. BNSF Railway
    c. 3M Company
    d. Supplemental Nutrition Assistance Program

Chapter 4. RECOGNIZING REVENUES IN GOVERNMENTAL FUNDS

34. An _____ is a practitioner of accountancy, which is the measurement, disclosure or provision of assurance about financial information that helps managers, investors, tax authorities and other decision makers make resource allocation decisions.

The word '_____' is derived from the French 'Compter' which took its origin from the Latin 'Computare'. The word was formerly written in English as 'Accomptant', but in process of time the word, which was always pronounced by dropping the 'p', became gradually changed both in pronunciation and in orthography to its present form.

a. Accountant
b. ABC Television Network
c. AMEX
d. AIG

35. The _____ is the global organization for the accountancy profession. IFAC has 157 member bodies and associates in 123 countries and jurisdictions, representing more than 2.5 million accountants employed in public practice, industry and commerce, government, and academe. The organization, through its independent standard-setting boards, establishes international standards on ethics, auditing and assurance, education, and public sector accounting.

a. Emerging technologies
b. International Accounting Standards Committee
c. American Payroll Association
d. International Federation of Accountants

36. _____ are payments made by a corporation to its shareholder members. It is the portion of corporate profits paid out to stockholders. When a corporation earns a profit or surplus, that money can be put to two uses: it can either be re-invested in the business (called retained earnings), or it can be paid to the shareholders as a dividend.

a. Dividends
b. Dividend payout ratio
c. Dividend stripping
d. Dividend yield

37. _____ is a fee paid on borrowed assets. It is the price paid for the use of borrowed money, or, money earned by deposited funds. Assets that are sometimes lent with _____ include money, shares, consumer goods through hire purchase, major assets such as aircraft, and even entire factories in finance lease arrangements. The _____ is calculated upon the value of the assets in the same manner as upon money.

a. Insolvency
b. ABC Television Network
c. AIG
d. Interest

38. _____ is that which is owed; usually referencing assets owed, but the term can also cover moral obligations and other interactions not requiring money. In the case of assets, _____ is a means of using future purchasing power in the present before a summation has been earned. Some companies and corporations use _____ as a part of their overall corporate finance strategy.

a. Lender
b. Loan
c. Debenture
d. Debt

Chapter 5. RECOGNIZING EXPENDITURES IN GOVERNMENTAL FUNDS   33

1. The _____ is the national, professional association of CPAs in the United States, with more than 330,000 members, including CPAs in business and industry, public practice, government, and education; student affiliates; and international associates. It sets ethical standards for the profession and U.S. auditing standards for audits of private companies; federal, state and local governments; and non-profit organizations.

Approximately 40% of its members are engaged in the practice of public accounting, in areas such as auditing, accounting, taxation, general business consulting, business valuation, personal financial planning and business technology.

   a. Other postemployment benefits
   b. ABC Television Network
   c. American Institute of Certified Public Accountants
   d. AIG

2. Project _____: The project _____ is a prediction of the costs associated with a particular company project. These costs include labor, materials, and other related expenses. The project _____ is often broken down into specific tasks, with task _____s assigned to each.
   a. BMC Software, Inc.
   b. BNSF Railway
   c. 3M Company
   d. Budget

3. The _____ is a federal agency within the legislative branch of the United States government. It is a government agency that provides economic data to Congress. It was created by the Congressional Budget and Impoundment Control Act of 1974.
   a. BMC Software, Inc.
   b. Congressional Budget Office
   c. General Accounting Office
   d. 3M Company

4. _____ is the term used to refer to the standard framework of guidelines for financial accounting used in any given jurisdiction. _____ includes the standards, conventions, and rules accountants follow in recording and summarizing transactions, and in the preparation of financial statements.

Financial accounting information must be assembled and reported objectively.

   a. General ledger
   b. Long-term liabilities
   c. Current asset
   d. Generally accepted accounting principles

5. The _____ is currently the source of generally accepted accounting principles (GAAP) used by State and Local governments in the [[United States of America]]. As with most of the entities involved in creating GAAP in the United States, it is a private, non-governmental organization.

The _____ is subject to oversight by the Financial Accounting Foundation (FAF), which selects the members of the _____ and the Financial Accounting Standards Board, and funds both organizations.

   a. Fannie Mae
   b. Governmental Accounting Standards Board
   c. National Conference of Commissioners on Uniform State Laws
   d. Multinational corporation

6. The _____ was established as the _____ by the Budget and Accounting Act of 1921 (Pub.L. 67-13, 42 Stat. 20, June 10, 1921.)

Chapter 5. RECOGNIZING EXPENDITURES IN GOVERNMENTAL FUNDS

a. BMC Software, Inc.
b. 3M Company
c. GAO
d. General Accounting Office

7. The word _____ indicates that a party, or proprietor, exercises private ownership, control or use over an item of property
   a. 3M Company
   b. BNSF Railway
   c. BMC Software, Inc.
   d. Proprietary

8. A _____ is a rest from work, a hiatus, typically lasting two or more months. The concept of a _____ has a source in several places in the Bible, where there is a commandment to desist from working the fields in the seventh year. In the strict sense therefore, a _____ lasts a year.
   a. 3M Company
   b. BNSF Railway
   c. BMC Software, Inc.
   d. Sabbatical

9. A _____ is a compensation, usually financial, received by a worker in exchange for their labor.

Compensation in terms of _____s is given to worker and compensation in terms of salary is given to employees. Compensation is a monetary benefits given to employees in returns of the services provided by them.

   a. BMC Software, Inc.
   b. 3M Company
   c. Retirement plan
   d. Wage

10. The _____ after Senator Harold Burton of Ohio and Senator Lister Hill of Alabama, is a United States federal law passed in 1946. This act responded to the first of Trumane;s proposals and was designed to provide federal grants and guaranteed loans to improve the physical plant of the natione;s hospital system. Money was designated to the states to achieve 4.5 beds per 1,000 people.
    a. Lease
    b. Hospital Survey and Construction Act
    c. Model Code of Professional Responsibility
    d. Tax patent

11. The _____ of a company or public agency is the corporate officer primarily responsible for managing the financial risks of the business or agency. This officer is also responsible for financial planning and record-keeping, as well as financial reporting to higher management. (In recent years, however, the role has expanded to encompass communicating financial performance and forecasts to the analyst community.)
    a. Chief Financial Officer
    b. Merck ' Co., Inc.
    c. Chief executive officer
    d. NASDAQ

12. The _____ signed into law by President George H.W. Bush on November 15, 1990, is a United States federal law intended to improve the government's financial management, outlining standards of financial performance and disclosure. Among other measures, the Office of Management and Budget (OMB) was given greater authority over federal financial management. For each of 23 federal departments and agencies, the position of chief financial officer was created.
    a. Bylaw
    b. Jenkins Committee
    c. Scottish Poor Laws
    d. Chief Financial Officers Act of 1990

Chapter 5. RECOGNIZING EXPENDITURES IN GOVERNMENTAL FUNDS 35

13. The _____ is a private, not-for-profit organization whose primary purpose is to develop generally accepted accounting principles (GAAP) within the United States in the public's interest. The Securities and Exchange Commission (SEC) designated the _____ as the organization responsible for setting accounting standards for public companies in the U.S. It was created in 1973, replacing the Accounting Principles Board and the Committee on Accounting Procedure of the American Institute of Certified Public Accountants. The _____'s mission is 'to establish and improve standards of financial accounting and reporting for the guidance and education of the public, including issuers, auditors, and users of financial information.'

The _____ is not a governmental body.

- a. Public company
- b. Financial Accounting Standards Board
- c. Governmental Accounting Standards Board
- d. Fannie Mae

14. The _____ is a Cabinet-level office, and is the largest office within the Executive Office of the President of the United States (EOP.) It is an important conduit by which the White House oversees the activities of federal agencies. OMB is tasked with giving expert advice to senior White House officials on a range of topics relating to federal policy, management, legislative, regulatory, and budgetary issues.

- a. Alaska Air Group
- b. AT'T Wireless Services, Inc.
- c. Analysis of variance
- d. Office of Management and Budget

15. A _____ is a pool of assets forming an independent legal entity that are bought with the contributions to a pension plan for the exclusive purpose of financing pension plan benefits.

_____s are important shareholders of listed and private companies. They are especially important to the stock market where large institutional investors like the Ontario Teachers' Pension Plan dominate.

- a. Pension fund
- b. Public offering
- c. Limited liability company
- d. Return on assets

16. The term _____ or superannuation refers to a pension granted upon retirement. They may be set up by employers, insurance companies, the government or other institutions such as employer associations or trade unions.

- a. 3M Company
- b. Wage
- c. BMC Software, Inc.
- d. Retirement plan

17. An _____ is a practitioner of accountancy, which is the measurement, disclosure or provision of assurance about financial information that helps managers, investors, tax authorities and other decision makers make resource allocation decisions.

The word '_____' is derived from the French 'Compter' which took its origin from the Latin 'Computare'. The word was formerly written in English as 'Accomptant', but in process of time the word, which was always pronounced by dropping the 'p', became gradually changed both in pronunciation and in orthography to its present form.

- a. ABC Television Network
- b. Accountant
- c. AMEX
- d. AIG

Chapter 5. RECOGNIZING EXPENDITURES IN GOVERNMENTAL FUNDS

18. The _____ is the global organization for the accountancy profession. IFAC has 157 member bodies and associates in 123 countries and jurisdictions, representing more than 2.5 million accountants employed in public practice, industry and commerce, government, and academe. The organization, through its independent standard-setting boards, establishes international standards on ethics,auditing and assurance, education, and public sector accounting.
   a. Emerging technologies
   b. American Payroll Association
   c. International Federation of Accountants
   d. International Accounting Standards Committee

19. _____ is the generic term that refers to all supplies regularly used in offices by businesses and other organizations, from private citizens to governments, who works with the collection, refinement, and output of information (colloquially referred to as 'paper work'.) _____ being sold at a drugstore. Hà Ná»™i's Stationery supplier

The term includes small, expendable, daily use items such as paper clips, staples, hole punches, binders and laminators, writing utensils and paper, but also encompasses higher-cost equipment like computers, printers, fax machines, photocopiers and cash registers, as well as office furniture such as cubicles or armoire desks. Two very common medium-to-high-cost office equipment items before the advent of suitably priced word processing machines and PCs in the 1970s and 1980s were typewriters and adding machines.

   a. Office supplies
   b. AMEX
   c. ABC Television Network
   d. AIG

20. The term _____ usually refers to a company that is permitted to offer its registered securities (stock, bonds, etc.) for sale to the general public, typically through a stock exchange, or occasionally a company whose stock is traded over the counter (OTC) via market makers who use non-exchange quotation services.

The term '_____' may also refer to a company owned by the government.

   a. Governmental Accounting Standards Board
   b. MicroStrategy
   c. Professional association
   d. Public Company

21. The _____ (sometimes called 'Peekaboo') is a private-sector, non-profit corporation created by the Sarbanes-Oxley Act, a 2002 United States federal law, to oversee the auditors of public companies. Its stated purpose is to 'protect the interests of investors and further the public interest in the preparation of informative, fair, and independent audit reports'. Although a private entity, the _____ has many government-like regulatory functions, making it in some ways similar to the private Self Regulatory Organizations (SROs) that regulate stock markets and other aspects of the financial markets in the United States.
   a. Pension Benefit Guaranty Corporation
   b. 3M Company
   c. Financial Crimes Enforcement Network
   d. Public Company Accounting Oversight Board

22. _____ refers to services paid for in advance. Examples include tolls, pay as you go cell phones, and stored-value cards such as gift cards and preloaded credit cards. _____ accounts are assets, and they are increased by debiting the account(s.)
   a. BNSF Railway
   b. BMC Software, Inc.
   c. 3M Company
   d. Prepaid

Chapter 5. RECOGNIZING EXPENDITURES IN GOVERNMENTAL FUNDS 37

23. In business and accounting, _____ are everything of value that is owned by a person or company. It is a claim on the property your income of a borrower. The balance sheet of a firm records the monetary value of the _____ owned by the firm.

   a. Earnings before interest, taxes, depreciation and amortization
   b. Accrual basis accounting
   c. Assets
   d. Accounts receivable

24. In economics, _____ or _____ goods or real _____ refers to factors of production used to create goods or services that are not themselves significantly consumed (though they may depreciate) in the production process. _____ goods may be acquired with money or financial _____. In finance and accounting, _____ generally refers to financial wealth, especially that used to start or maintain a business.

   a. Vyborg Appeal
   b. Screening
   c. Capital
   d. Disclosure

25. The term _____ has three unrelated technical definitions, and is also used in a variety of non-technical ways.

   - In financial economics, it refers to any asset used to make money, as opposed to assets used for personal enjoyment or consumption. This is an important distinction because two people can disagree sharply about the value of personal assets, one person might think a sports car is more valuable than a pickup truck, another person might have the opposite taste. But if an asset is held for the purpose of making money, taste has nothing to do with it, only differences of opinion about how much money the asset will produce. With the further assumption that people agree on the probability distribution of future cash flows, it is possible to have an objective _____ pricing model. Even without the assumption of agreement, it is possible to set rational limits on _____ value.
   - In governmental accounting, it is defined as any asset used in operations with an initial useful life extending beyond one reporting period. Generally, government managers have a 'stewardship' duty to maintain _____s under their control. See International Public Sector Accounting Standards for details.
   - In US tax accounting, it is defined as any property other than a list of exceptions. The main exceptions are anything held for sale, and any real estate or depreciable property used in business. Almost everything you own and use for personal purposes, pleasure or investment is a _____. If something is a _____ for tax purposes, gains or losses on sale or disposition are capital gains or capital losses. For individuals, however, capital losses on property held for personal use are generally not deductible. See the IRS publication Tax Facts about Capital Gains and Losses for details.

A well-known financial accounting textbook advises that the term be avoided except in tax accounting because it is used in so many different senses, not all of them well-defined. For example it is often used as a synonym for fixed assets or for investments in securities.

A common non-technical usage occurs when people ask that employees or the environment or something else be treated as a _____.

   a. BMC Software, Inc.
   b. Solvency
   c. Capital asset
   d. 3M Company

Chapter 5. RECOGNIZING EXPENDITURES IN GOVERNMENTAL FUNDS

26. _____ is that which is owed; usually referencing assets owed, but the term can also cover moral obligations and other interactions not requiring money. In the case of assets, _____ is a means of using future purchasing power in the present before a summation has been earned. Some companies and corporations use _____ as a part of their overall corporate finance strategy.
    a. Debenture
    b. Lender
    c. Loan
    d. Debt

27. _____ is a process by which a firm can obtain the use of a certain fixed assets for which it must pay a series of contractual, periodic, tax deductable payments. The lessee is the receiver of the services or the assets under the lease contract and the lessor is the owner of the assets. The relationship between the tenant and the landlord is called a tenancy, and can be for a fixed or an indefinite period of time (called the term of the lease.)
    a. Federal Sentencing Guidelines
    b. Property
    c. Resource Conservation and Recovery Act
    d. Leasing

28. _____ is a fee paid on borrowed assets. It is the price paid for the use of borrowed money , or, money earned by deposited funds .Assets that are sometimes lent with _____ include money, shares, consumer goods through hire purchase, major assets such as aircraft, and even entire factories in finance lease arrangements. The _____ is calculated upon the value of the assets in the same manner as upon money.
    a. AIG
    b. ABC Television Network
    c. Interest
    d. Insolvency

29. In finance, a _____ is a debt security, in which the authorized issuer owes the holders a debt and, depending on the terms of the _____, is obliged to pay interest (the coupon) and/or to repay the principal at a later date, termed maturity. It is a formal contract to repay borrowed money with interest at fixed intervals.

Thus a _____ is like a loan: the issuer is the borrower, the _____ holder is the lender, and the coupon is the interest.

    a. Zero-coupon bond
    b. Revenue bonds
    c. Coupon rate
    d. Bond

30. Discounting is a financial mechanism in which a debtor obtains the right to delay payments to a creditor, for a defined period of time, in exchange for a charge or fee. Essentially, the party that owes money in the present purchases the right to delay the payment until some future date. The _____, or charge, is simply the difference between the original amount owed in the present and the amount that has to be paid in the future to settle the debt.
    a. Discounting
    b. Discount
    c. Risk aversion
    d. Discount factor

31. _____ are payments made by a corporation to its shareholder members. It is the portion of corporate profits paid out to stockholders. When a corporation earns a profit or surplus, that money can be put to two uses: it can either be re-invested in the business (called retained earnings), or it can be paid to the shareholders as a dividend.
    a. Dividend stripping
    b. Dividends
    c. Dividend yield
    d. Dividend payout ratio

Chapter 5. RECOGNIZING EXPENDITURES IN GOVERNMENTAL FUNDS

32. In economic models, the _____ time frame assumes no fixed factors of production. Firms can enter or leave the marketplace, and the cost (and availability) of land, labor, raw materials, and capital goods can be assumed to vary. In contrast, in the short-run time frame, certain factors are assumed to be fixed, because there is not sufficient time for them to change.
   a. Short-run
   b. Long-run
   c. 3M Company
   d. BMC Software, Inc.

33. _____ is an accounting system often used by nonprofit organizations and by the public sector. According to StartHereGoPlaces, _____ is a '[m]ethod of accounting and presentation whereby assets and liabilities are grouped according to the purpose for which they are to be used.'

   _____ serves any nonprofit organization or the public sector. These organizations have a need for special reporting to financial statements users that show how money is spent, rather than how much profit was earned.

   a. Liquidating dividend
   b. Fund accounting
   c. Refunding
   d. Replacement cost

34. In accounting, _____ has a very specific meaning. It is an outflow of cash or other valuable assets from a person or company to another person or company. This outflow of cash is generally one side of a trade for products or services that have equal or better current or future value to the buyer than to the seller.
   a. ABC Television Network
   b. Expense
   c. AMEX
   d. AIG

35. _____ is an umbrella term which refers to the various accounting systems used by various public sector entities. In the United States, for instance, there are two levels of government which follow different accounting standards set forth by independent, private sector boards. At the federal level, the Federal Accounting Standards Advisory Board (FASAB) sets forth the accounting standards to follow.
   a. Product control
   b. Management accounting
   c. Nonassurance services
   d. Governmental Accounting

Chapter 6. ACCOUNTING FOR CAPITAL PROJECTS AND DEBT SERVICE

1. The _____ is the national, professional association of CPAs in the United States, with more than 330,000 members, including CPAs in business and industry, public practice, government, and education; student affiliates; and international associates. It sets ethical standards for the profession and U.S. auditing standards for audits of private companies; federal, state and local governments; and non-profit organizations.

   Approximately 40% of its members are engaged in the practice of public accounting, in areas such as auditing, accounting, taxation, general business consulting, business valuation, personal financial planning and business technology.

   a. Other postemployment benefits
   b. ABC Television Network
   c. AIG
   d. American Institute of Certified Public Accountants

2. Project _____: The project _____ is a prediction of the costs associated with a particular company project. These costs include labor, materials, and other related expenses. The project _____ is often broken down into specific tasks, with task _____s assigned to each.
   a. BNSF Railway
   b. BMC Software, Inc.
   c. 3M Company
   d. Budget

3. The _____ is a federal agency within the legislative branch of the United States government. It is a government agency that provides economic data to Congress. It was created by the Congressional Budget and Impoundment Control Act of 1974.
   a. General Accounting Office
   b. Congressional Budget Office
   c. BMC Software, Inc.
   d. 3M Company

4. The _____ is currently the source of generally accepted accounting principles (GAAP) used by State and Local governments in the [[United States of America]]. As with most of the entities involved in creating GAAP in the United States, it is a private, non-governmental organization.

   The _____ is subject to oversight by the Financial Accounting Foundation (FAF), which selects the members of the _____ and the Financial Accounting Standards Board, and funds both organizations.

   a. National Conference of Commissioners on Uniform State Laws
   b. Fannie Mae
   c. Multinational corporation
   d. Governmental Accounting Standards Board

5. The _____ was established as the _____ by the Budget and Accounting Act of 1921 (Pub.L. 67-13, 42 Stat. 20, June 10, 1921.)
   a. General Accounting Office
   b. GAO
   c. 3M Company
   d. BMC Software, Inc.

6. The term _____ usually refers to a company that is permitted to offer its registered securities (stock, bonds, etc.) for sale to the general public, typically through a stock exchange, or occasionally a company whose stock is traded over the counter (OTC) via market makers who use non-exchange quotation services.

   The term '_____' may also refer to a company owned by the government.

Chapter 6. ACCOUNTING FOR CAPITAL PROJECTS AND DEBT SERVICE

a. Governmental Accounting Standards Board
c. MicroStrategy
b. Public Company
d. Professional association

7. The _____ (sometimes called 'Peekaboo') is a private-sector, non-profit corporation created by the Sarbanes-Oxley Act, a 2002 United States federal law, to oversee the auditors of public companies. Its stated purpose is to 'protect the interests of investors and further the public interest in the preparation of informative, fair, and independent audit reports'. Although a private entity, the _____ has many government-like regulatory functions, making it in some ways similar to the private Self Regulatory Organizations (SROs) that regulate stock markets and other aspects of the financial markets in the United States.

a. 3M Company
c. Financial Crimes Enforcement Network
b. Public Company Accounting Oversight Board
d. Pension Benefit Guaranty Corporation

8. A _____ is a fungible, negotiable instrument representing financial value. they are broadly categorized into debt securities (such as banknotes, bonds and debentures), and equity securities; e.g., common stocks. The company or other entity issuing the _____ is called the issuer.

a. BMC Software, Inc.
c. Security
b. 3M Company
d. Tracking stock

9. _____ in the United States currently refers to the federal Old-Age, Survivors, and Disability Insurance (OASDI) program.

The original _____ Act and the current version of the Act, as amended encompass several social welfare and social insurance programs. The larger and better known programs are:

- Federal Old-Age, Survivors, and Disability Insurance
- Unemployment benefits
- Temporary Assistance for Needy Families
- Health Insurance for Aged and Disabled (Medicare)
- Grants to States for Medical Assistance Programs (Medicaid)
- State Children's Health Insurance Program (SCHIP)
- Supplemental Security Income (Social SecurityI)

U.S. _____ is a social insurance program funded through dedicated payroll taxes called Federal Insurance Contributions Act (FICA.) Tax deposits are formally entrusted to Federal Old-Age and Survivors Insurance Trust Fund, or Federal Disability Insurance Trust Fund, Federal Hospital Insurance Trust Fund or the Federal Supplementary Medical Insurance Trust Fund.

a. Social Security
c. Comparable
b. Sale
d. Price-to-sales ratio

10. The United States _____ is an independent agency of the United States federal government that administers Social Security, a social insurance program consisting of retirement, disability, and survivors' benefits. To qualify for these benefits, most American workers pay Social Security taxes on their earnings; future benefits are based on the employees' contributions.

The _____ was established by a law currently codified at 42 U.S.C.

a. Minority interest
b. Return on assets
c. Time value of money
d. Social Security Administration

11. In business and accounting, _____ are everything of value that is owned by a person or company. It is a claim on the property your income of a borrower. The balance sheet of a firm records the monetary value of the _____ owned by the firm.
   a. Assets
   b. Accounts receivable
   c. Accrual basis accounting
   d. Earnings before interest, taxes, depreciation and amortization

12. In economics, _____ or _____ goods or real _____ refers to factors of production used to create goods or services that are not themselves significantly consumed (though they may depreciate) in the production process. _____ goods may be acquired with money or financial _____. In finance and accounting, _____ generally refers to financial wealth, especially that used to start or maintain a business.
   a. Disclosure
   b. Vyborg Appeal
   c. Screening
   d. Capital

13. _____ is the term used to refer to the standard framework of guidelines for financial accounting used in any given jurisdiction. _____ includes the standards, conventions, and rules accountants follow in recording and summarizing transactions, and in the preparation of financial statements.

Financial accounting information must be assembled and reported objectively.

   a. Current asset
   b. General ledger
   c. Generally accepted accounting principles
   d. Long-term liabilities

14. The _____ after Senator Harold Burton of Ohio and Senator Lister Hill of Alabama, is a United States federal law passed in 1946. This act responded to the first of Trumane;s proposals and was designed to provide federal grants and guaranteed loans to improve the physical plant of the natione;s hospital system. Money was designated to the states to achieve 4.5 beds per 1,000 people.
   a. Tax patent
   b. Model Code of Professional Responsibility
   c. Lease
   d. Hospital Survey and Construction Act

15. In finance, a _____ is a debt security, in which the authorized issuer owes the holders a debt and, depending on the terms of the _____, is obliged to pay interest (the coupon) and/or to repay the principal at a later date, termed maturity. It is a formal contract to repay borrowed money with interest at fixed intervals.

Thus a _____ is like a loan: the issuer is the borrower, the _____ holder is the lender, and the coupon is the interest.

   a. Coupon rate
   b. Bond
   c. Revenue bonds
   d. Zero-coupon bond

Chapter 6. ACCOUNTING FOR CAPITAL PROJECTS AND DEBT SERVICE

16. Discounting is a financial mechanism in which a debtor obtains the right to delay payments to a creditor, for a defined period of time, in exchange for a charge or fee. Essentially, the party that owes money in the present purchases the right to delay the payment until some future date. The _____, or charge, is simply the difference between the original amount owed in the present and the amount that has to be paid in the future to settle the debt.
   a. Risk aversion
   b. Discount factor
   c. Discounting
   d. Discount

17. _____ are payments made by a corporation to its shareholder members. It is the portion of corporate profits paid out to stockholders. When a corporation earns a profit or surplus, that money can be put to two uses: it can either be re-invested in the business (called retained earnings), or it can be paid to the shareholders as a dividend.
   a. Dividend stripping
   b. Dividend payout ratio
   c. Dividend yield
   d. Dividends

18. _____ is a fee paid on borrowed assets. It is the price paid for the use of borrowed money, or, money earned by deposited funds. Assets that are sometimes lent with _____ include money, shares, consumer goods through hire purchase, major assets such as aircraft, and even entire factories in finance lease arrangements. The _____ is calculated upon the value of the assets in the same manner as upon money.
   a. AIG
   b. Insolvency
   c. ABC Television Network
   d. Interest

19. _____ is that which is owed; usually referencing assets owed, but the term can also cover moral obligations and other interactions not requiring money. In the case of assets, _____ is a means of using future purchasing power in the present before a summation has been earned. Some companies and corporations use _____ as a part of their overall corporate finance strategy.
   a. Loan
   b. Lender
   c. Debenture
   d. Debt

20. The term _____ has three unrelated technical definitions, and is also used in a variety of non-technical ways.

   - In financial economics, it refers to any asset used to make money, as opposed to assets used for personal enjoyment or consumption. This is an important distinction because two people can disagree sharply about the value of personal assets, one person might think a sports car is more valuable than a pickup truck, another person might have the opposite taste. But if an asset is held for the purpose of making money, taste has nothing to do with it, only differences of opinion about how much money the asset will produce. With the further assumption that people agree on the probability distribution of future cash flows, it is possible to have an objective _____ pricing model. Even without the assumption of agreement, it is possible to set rational limits on _____ value.
   - In governmental accounting, it is defined as any asset used in operations with an initial useful life extending beyond one reporting period. Generally, government managers have a 'stewardship' duty to maintain _____s under their control. See International Public Sector Accounting Standards for details.
   - In US tax accounting, it is defined as any property other than a list of exceptions. The main exceptions are anything held for sale, and any real estate or depreciable property used in business. Almost everything you own and use for personal purposes, pleasure or investment is a _____. If something is a _____ for tax purposes, gains or losses on sale or disposition are capital gains or capital losses. For individuals, however, capital losses on property held for personal use are generally not deductible. See the IRS publication Tax Facts about Capital Gains and Losses for details.

Chapter 6. ACCOUNTING FOR CAPITAL PROJECTS AND DEBT SERVICE

A well-known financial accounting textbook advises that the term be avoided except in tax accounting because it is used in so many different senses, not all of them well-defined. For example it is often used as a synonym for fixed assets or for investments in securities.

A common non-technical usage occurs when people ask that employees or the environment or something else be treated as a _____.

 a. 3M Company
 b. BMC Software, Inc.
 c. Solvency
 d. Capital asset

21. _____ is the term used in the United States to designate a unique charge government units can assess against real estate parcels for certain public projects. This charge is levied in a specific geographic area known as a _____ District (S.A.D.). A _____ may only be levied against parcels of real estate which have been identified as having received a direct and unique 'benefit' from the public project.Kadzban v City of Grandville, 502 N.W.2d 299, 501; Davies v City of Lawrence, 218 Kan.
 a. Malcolm Baldrige National Quality Award
 b. Fixed tax
 c. Tax Analysts
 d. Special assessment

22. The _____ is a Cabinet-level office, and is the largest office within the Executive Office of the President of the United States (EOP.) It is an important conduit by which the White House oversees the activities of federal agencies. OMB is tasked with giving expert advice to senior White House officials on a range of topics relating to federal policy, management, legislative, regulatory, and budgetary issues.
 a. AT'T Wireless Services, Inc.
 b. Alaska Air Group
 c. Office of Management and Budget
 d. Analysis of variance

23. In economics and finance, _____ is the practice of taking advantage of a price differential between two or more markets: striking a combination of matching deals that capitalize upon the imbalance, the profit being the difference between the market prices. When used by academics, an _____ is a transaction that involves no negative cash flow at any probabilistic or temporal state and a positive cash flow in at least one state; in simple terms, a risk-free profit. A person who engages in _____ is called an arbitrageur--such as a bank or brokerage firm.
 a. AIG
 b. ABC Television Network
 c. AMEX
 d. Arbitrage

24. _____ is an accounting system often used by nonprofit organizations and by the public sector. According to StartHereGoPlaces, _____ is a '[m]ethod of accounting and presentation whereby assets and liabilities are grouped according to the purpose for which they are to be used.'

_____ serves any nonprofit organization or the public sector. These organizations have a need for special reporting to financial statements users that show how money is spent, rather than how much profit was earned.

 a. Fund accounting
 b. Refunding
 c. Liquidating dividend
 d. Replacement cost

25. _____ is the process of changing the way taxes are collected or managed by the government.

Chapter 6. ACCOUNTING FOR CAPITAL PROJECTS AND DEBT SERVICE

_____ers have different goals. Some seek to reduce the level of taxation of all people by the government.

a. Tax exporting
c. Tax investigation
b. Tax Reform
d. Franchise tax

26. The U.S. Congress passed the _____, (Pub.L. 99-514, 100 Stat. 2085, enacted October 22, 1986) to simplify the income tax code, broaden the tax base and eliminate many tax shelters and other preferences.

The tax reform was designed to be revenue neutral, but because individual taxes were decreased while corporate taxes were increased, Congressional Budget Office estimates (which ignore corporate taxes) suggested every tax payer saw a decrease in their tax bill. As of 2009, the _____ was the most recent major simplification of the tax code, drastically reducing the number of deductions and the number of tax brackets.

a. 3M Company
c. Tax Reform Act of 1986
b. BMC Software, Inc.
d. BNSF Railway

27. _____ refers to the replacement of an existing debt obligation with a debt obligation bearing different terms. The most common consumer _____ is for a home mortgage.

_____ may be undertaken to reduce interest rate/interest costs (by _____ at a lower rate), to extend the repayment time, to pay off other debt(s), to reduce one's periodic payment obligations (sometimes by taking a longer-term loan), to reduce or alter risk (such as by _____ from a variable-rate to a fixed-rate loan), and/or to raise cash for investment, consumption, or the payment of a dividend.

a. BMC Software, Inc.
c. BNSF Railway
b. 3M Company
d. Refinancing

28. _____ occurs when an entity that has issued callable bonds calls those debt securities from the debt holders with the express purpose of reissuing new debt at a lower coupon rate. In essence, the issue of new, lower-interest debt allows the company to prematurely refund the older, higher-interest debt.

On the contrary, NonRefundable Bonds may be callable but they cannot be re-issued with a lower coupon rate.

a. Lump sum
c. Redemption value
b. Refunding
d. Manufacturing operations

Chapter 7. LONG-LIVED ASSETS AND INVESTMENTS IN MARKETABLE SECURITIES

1. The _____ is the national, professional association of CPAs in the United States, with more than 330,000 members, including CPAs in business and industry, public practice, government, and education; student affiliates; and international associates. It sets ethical standards for the profession and U.S. auditing standards for audits of private companies; federal, state and local governments; and non-profit organizations.

Approximately 40% of its members are engaged in the practice of public accounting, in areas such as auditing, accounting, taxation, general business consulting, business valuation, personal financial planning and business technology.

   a. ABC Television Network
   b. AIG
   c. Other postemployment benefits
   d. American Institute of Certified Public Accountants

2. An _____ is a practitioner of accountancy, which is the measurement, disclosure or provision of assurance about financial information that helps managers, investors, tax authorities and other decision makers make resource allocation decisions.

The word '_____' is derived from the French 'Compter' which took its origin from the Latin 'Computare'. The word was formerly written in English as 'Accomptant', but in process of time the word, which was always pronounced by dropping the 'p', became gradually changed both in pronunciation and in orthography to its present form.

   a. Accountant
   b. AMEX
   c. ABC Television Network
   d. AIG

3. Project _____: The project _____ is a prediction of the costs associated with a particular company project. These costs include labor, materials, and other related expenses. The project _____ is often broken down into specific tasks, with task _____s assigned to each.
   a. Budget
   b. 3M Company
   c. BMC Software, Inc.
   d. BNSF Railway

4. The _____ is a federal agency within the legislative branch of the United States government. It is a government agency that provides economic data to Congress. It was created by the Congressional Budget and Impoundment Control Act of 1974.
   a. 3M Company
   b. General Accounting Office
   c. BMC Software, Inc.
   d. Congressional Budget Office

5. The _____ is a private, not-for-profit organization whose primary purpose is to develop generally accepted accounting principles (GAAP) within the United States in the public's interest. The Securities and Exchange Commission (SEC) designated the _____ as the organization responsible for setting accounting standards for public companies in the U.S. It was created in 1973, replacing the Accounting Principles Board and the Committee on Accounting Procedure of the American Institute of Certified Public Accountants. The _____'s mission is 'to establish and improve standards of financial accounting and reporting for the guidance and education of the public, including issuers, auditors, and users of financial information.'

The _____ is not a governmental body.

Chapter 7. LONG-LIVED ASSETS AND INVESTMENTS IN MARKETABLE SECURITIES

a. Governmental Accounting Standards Board
b. Fannie Mae
c. Public company
d. Financial Accounting Standards Board

6. The _____ is currently the source of generally accepted accounting principles (GAAP) used by State and Local governments in the [[United States of America]]. As with most of the entities involved in creating GAAP in the United States, it is a private, non-governmental organization.

The _____ is subject to oversight by the Financial Accounting Foundation (FAF), which selects the members of the _____ and the Financial Accounting Standards Board, and funds both organizations.

a. National Conference of Commissioners on Uniform State Laws
b. Fannie Mae
c. Governmental Accounting Standards Board
d. Multinational corporation

7. The _____ is the global organization for the accountancy profession. IFAC has 157 member bodies and associates in 123 countries and jurisdictions, representing more than 2.5 million accountants employed in public practice, industry and commerce, government, and academe. The organization, through its independent standard-setting boards, establishes international standards on ethics, auditing and assurance, education, and public sector accounting.

a. International Federation of Accountants
b. American Payroll Association
c. Emerging technologies
d. International Accounting Standards Committee

8. In business and accounting, _____ are everything of value that is owned by a person or company. It is a claim on the property your income of a borrower. The balance sheet of a firm records the monetary value of the _____ owned by the firm.

a. Accounts receivable
b. Accrual basis accounting
c. Earnings before interest, taxes, depreciation and amortization
d. Assets

9. In economics, _____ or _____ goods or real _____ refers to factors of production used to create goods or services that are not themselves significantly consumed (though they may depreciate) in the production process. _____ goods may be acquired with money or financial _____. In finance and accounting, _____ generally refers to financial wealth, especially that used to start or maintain a business.

a. Screening
b. Disclosure
c. Vyborg Appeal
d. Capital

Chapter 7. LONG-LIVED ASSETS AND INVESTMENTS IN MARKETABLE SECURITIES

10. The term _____ has three unrelated technical definitions, and is also used in a variety of non-technical ways.

    - In financial economics, it refers to any asset used to make money, as opposed to assets used for personal enjoyment or consumption. This is an important distinction because two people can disagree sharply about the value of personal assets, one person might think a sports car is more valuable than a pickup truck, another person might have the opposite taste. But if an asset is held for the purpose of making money, taste has nothing to do with it, only differences of opinion about how much money the asset will produce. With the further assumption that people agree on the probability distribution of future cash flows, it is possible to have an objective _____ pricing model. Even without the assumption of agreement, it is possible to set rational limits on _____ value.
    - In governmental accounting, it is defined as any asset used in operations with an initial useful life extending beyond one reporting period. Generally, government managers have a 'stewardship' duty to maintain _____s under their control. See International Public Sector Accounting Standards for details.
    - In US tax accounting, it is defined as any property other than a list of exceptions. The main exceptions are anything held for sale, and any real estate or depreciable property used in business. Almost everything you own and use for personal purposes, pleasure or investment is a _____. If something is a _____ for tax purposes, gains or losses on sale or disposition are capital gains or capital losses. For individuals, however, capital losses on property held for personal use are generally not deductible. See the IRS publication Tax Facts about Capital Gains and Losses for details.

A well-known financial accounting textbook advises that the term be avoided except in tax accounting because it is used in so many different senses, not all of them well-defined. For example it is often used as a synonym for fixed assets or for investments in securities.

A common non-technical usage occurs when people ask that employees or the environment or something else be treated as a _____.

a. Solvency
b. Capital asset
c. BMC Software, Inc.
d. 3M Company

11. _____ is a term used in accounting, economics and finance to spread the cost of an asset over the span of several years.

In simple words we can say that _____ is the reduction in the value of an asset due to usage, passage of time, wear and tear, technological outdating or obsolescence, depletion, inadequacy, rot, rust, decay or other such factors.

In accounting, _____ is a term used to describe any method of attributing the historical or purchase cost of an asset across its useful life, roughly corresponding to normal wear and tear.

a. General ledger
b. Current asset
c. Net profit
d. Depreciation

12. _____ are securities that can be easily converted into cash. Such securities will generally have highly liquid markets allowing the security to be sold at a reasonable price very quickly. This is a usual feature in real estate .

Chapter 7. LONG-LIVED ASSETS AND INVESTMENTS IN MARKETABLE SECURITIES

a. 3M Company
c. BMC Software, Inc.
b. Tracking stock
d. Marketable

13. A _____ is a fungible, negotiable instrument representing financial value. they are broadly categorized into debt securities (such as banknotes, bonds and debentures), and equity securities; e.g., common stocks. The company or other entity issuing the _____ is called the issuer.
   a. Security
   c. Tracking stock
   b. BMC Software, Inc.
   d. 3M Company

14. The _____ of a company or public agency is the corporate officer primarily responsible for managing the financial risks of the business or agency. This officer is also responsible for financial planning and record-keeping, as well as financial reporting to higher management. (In recent years, however, the role has expanded to encompass communicating financial performance and forecasts to the analyst community.)
   a. Chief executive officer
   c. NASDAQ
   b. Merck ' Co., Inc.
   d. Chief Financial Officer

15. The _____ signed into law by President George H.W. Bush on November 15, 1990, is a United States federal law intended to improve the government's financial management, outlining standards of financial performance and disclosure. Among other measures, the Office of Management and Budget (OMB) was given greater authority over federal financial management. For each of 23 federal departments and agencies, the position of chief financial officer was created.
   a. Chief Financial Officers Act of 1990
   c. Scottish Poor Laws
   b. Jenkins Committee
   d. Bylaw

16. The _____ after Senator Harold Burton of Ohio and Senator Lister Hill of Alabama, is a United States federal law passed in 1946. This act responded to the first of Trumane;s proposals and was designed to provide federal grants and guaranteed loans to improve the physical plant of the natione;s hospital system. Money was designated to the states to achieve 4.5 beds per 1,000 people.
   a. Lease
   c. Tax patent
   b. Model Code of Professional Responsibility
   d. Hospital Survey and Construction Act

17. A _____ is an administrative entity composed of a clearly defined territory and its population and commonly denotes a city, town or a small grouping of them. A _____ is typically governed by a mayor and a city council or municipal council.

The notion of _____ includes townships but is not restricted to them.

   a. 3M Company
   c. Municipality
   b. BMC Software, Inc.
   d. BNSF Railway

18. _____, in accrual accounting, is any account where the asset or liability is not realized until a future date (accounting period), e.g. annuities, charges, taxes, income, etc. The _____ item may be carried, dependent on type of deferral, as either an asset or liability.
   a. Cash basis accounting
   c. Payroll
   b. Pro forma
   d. Deferred

Chapter 7. LONG-LIVED ASSETS AND INVESTMENTS IN MARKETABLE SECURITIES

19. _____ is the practice of postponing maintenance activities such as repairs on both real property (i.e. infrastructure) and personal property (i.e. machinery) in order to save costs, meet budget funding levels, or realign available budget monies. The failure to perform needed repairs could lead to asset deterioration and ultimately asset impairment. Generally, a policy of continued _____ may result in higher costs, asset failure, and in some cases, health and safety implications.
   a. BMC Software, Inc.
   b. 3M Company
   c. BNSF Railway
   d. Deferred maintenance

20. _____ are formal records of a business' financial activities.

   In British English, including United Kingdom company law, _____ are often referred to as accounts, although the term _____ is also used, particularly by accountants.

   _____ provide an overview of a business' financial condition in both short and long term.

   a. Financial statements
   b. Statement of retained earnings
   c. Notes to the financial statements
   d. 3M Company

21. _____ are defined as identifiable non-monetary assets that cannot be seen, touched or physically measured, which are created through time and/or effort and that are identifiable as a separate asset. There are two primary forms of intangibles - legal intangibles (such as trade secrets (e.g., customer lists), copyrights, patents, trademarks, and goodwill) and competitive intangibles (such as knowledge activities (know-how, knowledge), collaboration activities, leverage activities, and structural activities.) Legal intangibles are known under the generic term intellectual property and generate legal property rights defensible in a court of law.
   a. Intangible assets
   b. ABC Television Network
   c. Overhead
   d. AIG

22. The term _____ usually refers to a company that is permitted to offer its registered securities (stock, bonds, etc.) for sale to the general public, typically through a stock exchange, or occasionally a company whose stock is traded over the counter (OTC) via market makers who use non-exchange quotation services.

   The term '_____' may also refer to a company owned by the government.

   a. MicroStrategy
   b. Governmental Accounting Standards Board
   c. Professional association
   d. Public Company

23. The _____ (sometimes called 'Peekaboo') is a private-sector, non-profit corporation created by the Sarbanes-Oxley Act, a 2002 United States federal law, to oversee the auditors of public companies. Its stated purpose is to 'protect the interests of investors and further the public interest in the preparation of informative, fair, and independent audit reports'. Although a private entity, the _____ has many government-like regulatory functions, making it in some ways similar to the private Self Regulatory Organizations (SROs) that regulate stock markets and other aspects of the financial markets in the United States.
   a. Financial Crimes Enforcement Network
   b. 3M Company
   c. Pension Benefit Guaranty Corporation
   d. Public Company Accounting Oversight Board

Chapter 7. LONG-LIVED ASSETS AND INVESTMENTS IN MARKETABLE SECURITIES

24. A _____ allows a borrower to use a financial security as collateral for a cash loan at a fixed rate of interest. In a repo, the borrower agrees to sell immediately a security to a lender and also agrees to buy the same security from the lender at a fixed price at some later date. A repo is equivalent to a cash transaction combined with a forward contract.
    a. 3M Company
    b. BMC Software, Inc.
    c. BNSF Railway
    d. Repurchase agreement

25. Depending on the nature of the investment, the type of _____ will vary.

A common concern with any investment is that you may lose the money you invest - your capital. This risk is therefore often referred to as 'capital risk.'

If the assets you invest in are held in another currency there is a risk that currency movements alone may affect the value.

    a. AMEX
    b. AIG
    c. ABC Television Network
    d. Investment risk

26. _____ is a concept that denotes the precise probability of specific eventualities. Technically, the notion of _____ is independent from the notion of value and, as such, eventualities may have both beneficial and adverse consequences. However, in general usage the convention is to focus only on potential negative impact to some characteristic of value that may arise from a future event.
    a. Discount factor
    b. Risk adjusted return on capital
    c. Discounting
    d. Risk

Chapter 7. LONG-LIVED ASSETS AND INVESTMENTS IN MARKETABLE SECURITIES

27. _____ means the giving out of information, either voluntarily or to be in compliance with legal regulations or workplace rules.

- In Computer security, full _____ means disclosing full information about vulnerabilities.
- In computing, _____ widget
- Journalism, full _____ refers to disclosing the interests of the writer which may bear on the subject being written about, for example, if the writer has worked with an interview subject in the past.

- In law:
    - The law of England and Wales, _____ refers to a process that may form part of legal proceedings, whereby parties inform to other parties the existence of any relevant documents that are, or have been, in their control. This compares with the process known as discovery in the course of legal proceedings in the United States.
    - In U.S. civil procedure (litigation rules for civil cases), _____ is a stage prior to trial. In civil cases, each party must disclose to the opposing party the following: names of witnesses which it may use to support its side, copies of documents (or mere description of these documents) in its control which it may use to support its side, computation of damages claimed, and certain insurance information. _____ is related to, but technically prior to, the discovery stage.
    - In Company law (known as 'corporate law' in the United States), _____ refers to giving out information about public or limited companies or their officers, which might be kept secret if the company was a private company or a partnership.

- In real property transactions, _____ refers to providing to a buyer information known to the seller or broker/agent concerning the condition or other aspects of real property that would affect the property's value or desirability. These rules regarding what information must be disclosed, and whether the information must be disclosed even if a buyer does not ask, vary from one jurisdiction to the next.

a. Tax harmonisation
b. Disclosure
c. Controlled Foreign Corporations
d. Trailing

28. The _____ was established as the _____ by the Budget and Accounting Act of 1921 (Pub.L. 67-13, 42 Stat. 20, June 10, 1921.)
a. BMC Software, Inc.
b. GAO
c. 3M Company
d. General Accounting Office

29. _____ is a legally declared inability or impairment of ability of an individual or organization to pay its creditors. Creditors may file a _____ petition against a debtor ('involuntary _____') in an effort to recoup a portion of what they are owed or initiate a restructuring. In the majority of cases, however, _____ is initiated by the debtor (a 'voluntary _____' that is filed by the bankrupt individual or organization.)
a. 3M Company
b. Bankruptcy protection
c. BMC Software, Inc.
d. Bankruptcy

Chapter 8. LONG-TERM OBLIGATIONS

1. The _____ is the national, professional association of CPAs in the United States, with more than 330,000 members, including CPAs in business and industry, public practice, government, and education; student affiliates; and international associates. It sets ethical standards for the profession and U.S. auditing standards for audits of private companies; federal, state and local governments; and non-profit organizations.

   Approximately 40% of its members are engaged in the practice of public accounting, in areas such as auditing, accounting, taxation, general business consulting, business valuation, personal financial planning and business technology.

   a. Other postemployment benefits
   b. ABC Television Network
   c. AIG
   d. American Institute of Certified Public Accountants

2. The _____ is a private, not-for-profit organization whose primary purpose is to develop generally accepted accounting principles (GAAP) within the United States in the public's interest. The Securities and Exchange Commission (SEC) designated the _____ as the organization responsible for setting accounting standards for public companies in the U.S. It was created in 1973, replacing the Accounting Principles Board and the Committee on Accounting Procedure of the American Institute of Certified Public Accountants. The _____'s mission is 'to establish and improve standards of financial accounting and reporting for the guidance and education of the public, including issuers, auditors, and users of financial information.'

   The _____ is not a governmental body.

   a. Fannie Mae
   b. Public company
   c. Financial Accounting Standards Board
   d. Governmental Accounting Standards Board

3. The _____ was established as the _____ by the Budget and Accounting Act of 1921 (Pub.L. 67-13, 42 Stat. 20, June 10, 1921.)
   a. BMC Software, Inc.
   b. GAO
   c. General Accounting Office
   d. 3M Company

4. A _____ is a fungible, negotiable instrument representing financial value. they are broadly categorized into debt securities (such as banknotes, bonds and debentures), and equity securities; e.g., common stocks. The company or other entity issuing the _____ is called the issuer.
   a. Tracking stock
   b. BMC Software, Inc.
   c. 3M Company
   d. Security

5. _____ in the United States currently refers to the federal Old-Age, Survivors, and Disability Insurance (OASDI) program.

Chapter 8. LONG-TERM OBLIGATIONS

The original _____ Act and the current version of the Act, as amended encompass several social welfare and social insurance programs. The larger and better known programs are:

- Federal Old-Age, Survivors, and Disability Insurance
- Unemployment benefits
- Temporary Assistance for Needy Families
- Health Insurance for Aged and Disabled (Medicare)
- Grants to States for Medical Assistance Programs (Medicaid)
- State Children's Health Insurance Program (SCHIP)
- Supplemental Security Income (Social SecurityI)

U.S. _____ is a social insurance program funded through dedicated payroll taxes called Federal Insurance Contributions Act (FICA.) Tax deposits are formally entrusted to Federal Old-Age and Survivors Insurance Trust Fund, or Federal Disability Insurance Trust Fund, Federal Hospital Insurance Trust Fund or the Federal Supplementary Medical Insurance Trust Fund.

   a. Sale
   c. Price-to-sales ratio
   b. Comparable
   d. Social Security

6. The United States _____ is an independent agency of the United States federal government that administers Social Security, a social insurance program consisting of retirement, disability, and survivors' benefits. To qualify for these benefits, most American workers pay Social Security taxes on their earnings; future benefits are based on the employees' contributions.

The _____ was established by a law currently codified at 42 U.S.C.

   a. Return on assets
   c. Minority interest
   b. Time value of money
   d. Social Security Administration

7. _____ is a legally declared inability or impairment of ability of an individual or organization to pay its creditors. Creditors may file a _____ petition against a debtor ('involuntary _____') in an effort to recoup a portion of what they are owed or initiate a restructuring. In the majority of cases, however, _____ is initiated by the debtor (a 'voluntary _____' that is filed by the bankrupt individual or organization.)
   a. BMC Software, Inc.
   c. Bankruptcy protection
   b. 3M Company
   d. Bankruptcy

8. _____ is that which is owed; usually referencing assets owed, but the term can also cover moral obligations and other interactions not requiring money. In the case of assets, _____ is a means of using future purchasing power in the present before a summation has been earned. Some companies and corporations use _____ as a part of their overall corporate finance strategy.
   a. Debt
   c. Lender
   b. Debenture
   d. Loan

Chapter 8. LONG-TERM OBLIGATIONS

9. A _____ is a type of debt Like all debt instruments, a _____ entails the redistribution of financial assets over time, between the lender and the borrower.
   a. Loan to value
   b. Loan
   c. Debenture
   d. Lender

10. In economic models, the _____ time frame assumes no fixed factors of production. Firms can enter or leave the marketplace, and the cost (and availability) of land, labor, raw materials, and capital goods can be assumed to vary. In contrast, in the short-run time frame, certain factors are assumed to be fixed, because there is not sufficient time for them to change.
   a. 3M Company
   b. Long-run
   c. BMC Software, Inc.
   d. Short-run

11. Project _____: The project _____ is a prediction of the costs associated with a particular company project. These costs include labor, materials, and other related expenses. The project _____ is often broken down into specific tasks, with task _____s assigned to each.
   a. BMC Software, Inc.
   b. 3M Company
   c. BNSF Railway
   d. Budget

12. The _____ is a federal agency within the legislative branch of the United States government. It is a government agency that provides economic data to Congress. It was created by the Congressional Budget and Impoundment Control Act of 1974.
   a. BMC Software, Inc.
   b. 3M Company
   c. General Accounting Office
   d. Congressional Budget Office

13. The _____ after Senator Harold Burton of Ohio and Senator Lister Hill of Alabama, is a United States federal law passed in 1946. This act responded to the first of Trumane;s proposals and was designed to provide federal grants and guaranteed loans to improve the physical plant of the natione;s hospital system. Money was designated to the states to achieve 4.5 beds per 1,000 people.
   a. Model Code of Professional Responsibility
   b. Lease
   c. Hospital Survey and Construction Act
   d. Tax patent

14. _____ is the term used to refer to the standard framework of guidelines for financial accounting used in any given jurisdiction. _____ includes the standards, conventions, and rules accountants follow in recording and summarizing transactions, and in the preparation of financial statements.

Financial accounting information must be assembled and reported objectively.

   a. Current asset
   b. Generally accepted accounting principles
   c. General ledger
   d. Long-term liabilities

15. _____ is an umbrella term which refers to the various accounting systems used by various public sector entities. In the United States, for instance, there are two levels of government which follow different accounting standards set forth by independent, private sector boards. At the federal level, the Federal Accounting Standards Advisory Board (FASAB) sets forth the accounting standards to follow.

Chapter 8. LONG-TERM OBLIGATIONS

a. Product control
b. Management accounting
c. Nonassurance services
d. Governmental Accounting

16. The _____ is currently the source of generally accepted accounting principles (GAAP) used by State and Local governments in the [[United States of America]]. As with most of the entities involved in creating GAAP in the United States, it is a private, non-governmental organization.

The _____ is subject to oversight by the Financial Accounting Foundation (FAF), which selects the members of the _____ and the Financial Accounting Standards Board, and funds both organizations.

a. Governmental Accounting Standards Board
b. Multinational corporation
c. Fannie Mae
d. National Conference of Commissioners on Uniform State Laws

17. In finance, a _____ is a debt security, in which the authorized issuer owes the holders a debt and, depending on the terms of the _____, is obliged to pay interest (the coupon) and/or to repay the principal at a later date, termed maturity. It is a formal contract to repay borrowed money with interest at fixed intervals.

Thus a _____ is like a loan: the issuer is the borrower, the _____ holder is the lender, and the coupon is the interest.

a. Zero-coupon bond
b. Revenue bonds
c. Coupon rate
d. Bond

18. An _____ is a practitioner of accountancy, which is the measurement, disclosure or provision of assurance about financial information that helps managers, investors, tax authorities and other decision makers make resource allocation decisions.

The word '_____' is derived from the French 'Compter' which took its origin from the Latin 'Computare'. The word was formerly written in English as 'Accomptant', but in process of time the word, which was always pronounced by dropping the 'p', became gradually changed both in pronunciation and in orthography to its present form.

a. AMEX
b. Accountant
c. ABC Television Network
d. AIG

19. The _____ is the global organization for the accountancy profession. IFAC has 157 member bodies and associates in 123 countries and jurisdictions, representing more than 2.5 million accountants employed in public practice, industry and commerce, government, and academe. The organization, through its independent standard-setting boards, establishes international standards on ethics,auditing and assurance, education, and public sector accounting.

a. International Accounting Standards Committee
b. Emerging technologies
c. American Payroll Association
d. International Federation of Accountants

Chapter 8. LONG-TERM OBLIGATIONS

20. A _____ is any one of a variety of different systems, institutions, procedures, social relations and infrastructures whereby persons trade, and goods and services are exchanged, forming part of the economy. It is an arrangement that allows buyers and sellers to exchange things. _____s vary in size, range, geographic scale, location, types and variety of human communities, as well as the types of goods and services traded.
   a. Recession
   b. Market
   c. Market Failure
   d. Perfect competition

21. _____ is the price at which an asset would trade in a competitive Walrasian auction setting. _____ is often used interchangeably with open _____, fair value or fair _____, although these terms have distinct definitions in different standards, and may differ in some circumstances.

International Valuation Standards defines _____ as 'the estimated amount for which a property should exchange on the date of valuation between a willing buyer and a willing seller in an arme;s-length transaction after proper marketing wherein the parties had each acted knowledgeably, prudently, and without compulsion.'

_____ is a concept distinct from market price, which is e;the price at which one can transacte;, while _____ is e;the true underlying valuee; according to theoretical standards.

   a. Debtor
   b. Segregated portfolio company
   c. Sinking fund
   d. Market value

22. _____ is the value on a given date of a future payment or series of future payments, discounted to reflect the time value of money and other factors such as investment risk. _____ calculations are widely used in business and economics to provide a means to compare cash flows at different times on a meaningful 'like to like' basis.

The most commonly applied model of the time value of money is compound interest.

   a. 3M Company
   b. Net present value
   c. Future value
   d. Present value

23. The _____ is a Cabinet-level office, and is the largest office within the Executive Office of the President of the United States (EOP.) It is an important conduit by which the White House oversees the activities of federal agencies. OMB is tasked with giving expert advice to senior White House officials on a range of topics relating to federal policy, management, legislative, regulatory, and budgetary issues.
   a. Alaska Air Group
   b. Analysis of variance
   c. AT'T Wireless Services, Inc.
   d. Office of Management and Budget

24. In economics, _____ or _____ goods or real _____ refers to factors of production used to create goods or services that are not themselves significantly consumed (though they may depreciate) in the production process. _____ goods may be acquired with money or financial _____. In finance and accounting, _____ generally refers to financial wealth, especially that used to start or maintain a business.
   a. Screening
   b. Vyborg Appeal
   c. Disclosure
   d. Capital

Chapter 8. LONG-TERM OBLIGATIONS

25. _____ is a type of lease - the other being an operating lease. A _____ effectively allows a firm to finance the purchase of an asset, even if, strictly speaking, the firm never acquires the asset. Typically, a _____ will give the lessee control over an asset for a large proportion of the asset's useful life, providing them the benefits and risks of ownership.
    a. Finance lease
    b. Profitability index
    c. Debt ratio
    d. 3M Company

26. In economics, business, retail, and accounting, a _____ is the value of money that has been used up to produce something, and hence is not available for use anymore. In economics, a _____ is an alternative that is given up as a result of a decision. In business, the _____ may be one of acquisition, in which case the amount of money expended to acquire it is counted as _____.
    a. Cost allocation
    b. Cost of quality
    c. Prime cost
    d. Cost

27. A _____ is a contract conferring a right on one person to possess property belonging to another person (called a landlord or lessor) to the exclusion of the owner landlord. It is a rental agreement between landlord and tenant. The relationship between the tenant and the landlord is called a tenancy, and the right to possession by the tenant is sometimes called a leasehold interest.
    a. Robinson-Patman Act
    b. Model Code of Professional Responsibility
    c. Federal Sentencing Guidelines
    d. Lease

28. _____ is a process by which a firm can obtain the use of a certain fixed assets for which it must pay a series of contractual, periodic, tax deductable payments. The lessee is the receiver of the services or the assets under the lease contract and the lessor is the owner of the assets. The relationship between the tenant and the landlord is called a tenancy, and can be for a fixed or an indefinite period of time (called the term of the lease.)
    a. Federal Sentencing Guidelines
    b. Resource Conservation and Recovery Act
    c. Property
    d. Leasing

29. _____s are the recurring expenses which are related to the operation of a business component, piece of equipment or facility.

For a commercial enterprise, _____s fall into two broad categories:

- fixed costs, which are the same whether the operation is closed or running at 100% capacity
- variable costs, which may increase depending on whether more production is done, and how it is done (producing 100 items of product might require 10 days of normal time or take 7 days if overtime is used. It may be more or less expensive to use overtime production depending on whether faster production means the product can be more profitable.)

Overhead costs for a business are the cost of resources used by an organization just to maintain its existence. Overhead costs are usually measured in monetary terms, but non-monetary overhead is possible in the form of time required to accomplish tasks.

Chapter 8. LONG-TERM OBLIGATIONS

Examples of overhead costs include:

- payment of rent on the office space a business occupies
- cost of electricity for the office lights
- some office personnel wages

Non-overhead costs are incremental costs, such as the cost of raw materials used in the goods a business sells.

In the case of a device, component, piece of equipment or facility (for the rest of this article, all of these items will be referred to in general as equipment), it is the regular, usual and customary recurring costs of operating the equipment.

a. AMEX
c. ABC Television Network
b. AIG
d. Operating cost

30. A _____ is a legal pledge in United States municipal finance, in which an entity pledges its full faith and credit to repay its debt, typically a _____ bond.
   a. Negligence
   c. Hospital Survey and Construction Act
   b. Letter of credit
   d. General obligation

31. _____ are bonds issued by governments, authorities, or public benefit corporations that are guaranteed by the revenue flow of the issuing agency.

The Supreme Court decision of Pollock versus Farmer's Loan and Trust Company of 1895 initiated a wave or series of innovations for the financial services community in both tax-treatment and regulation from government. This specific case, according to a leading investment bank's research, resulted in the 'intergovernmental tax immunity doctrine,' ultimately leading to 'tax-free status.' Municipal bonds are generally exempt from federal tax on their interest payments (not capital gains.)

a. Zero-coupon bond
c. Revenue bonds
b. Municipal bond
d. Callable bond

Chapter 8. LONG-TERM OBLIGATIONS

32. _____ means the giving out of information, either voluntarily or to be in compliance with legal regulations or workplace rules.

- In Computer security, full _____ means disclosing full information about vulnerabilities.
- In computing, _____ widget
- Journalism, full _____ refers to disclosing the interests of the writer which may bear on the subject being written about, for example, if the writer has worked with an interview subject in the past.

- In law:
    - The law of England and Wales, _____ refers to a process that may form part of legal proceedings, whereby parties inform to other parties the existence of any relevant documents that are, or have been, in their control. This compares with the process known as discovery in the course of legal proceedings in the United States.
    - In U.S. civil procedure (litigation rules for civil cases), _____ is a stage prior to trial. In civil cases, each party must disclose to the opposing party the following: names of witnesses which it may use to support its side, copies of documents (or mere description of these documents) in its control which it may use to support its side, computation of damages claimed, and certain insurance information. _____ is related to, but technically prior to, the discovery stage.
    - In Company law (known as 'corporate law' in the United States), _____ refers to giving out information about public or limited companies or their officers, which might be kept secret if the company was a private company or a partnership.

- In real property transactions, _____ refers to providing to a buyer information known to the seller or broker/agent concerning the condition or other aspects of real property that would affect the property's value or desirability. These rules regarding what information must be disclosed, and whether the information must be disclosed even if a buyer does not ask, vary from one jurisdiction to the next.

a. Tax harmonisation
c. Trailing
b. Controlled Foreign Corporations
d. Disclosure

33. _____, in law and economics, is a form of risk management primarily used to hedge against the risk of a contingent loss. _____ is defined as the equitable transfer of the risk of a loss, from one entity to another, in exchange for a premium, and can be thought of as a guaranteed small loss to prevent a large, possibly devastating loss. An insurer is a company selling the _____; an insured is the person or entity buying the _____.

a. AMEX
c. ABC Television Network
b. AIG
d. Insurance

34. In financial accounting, a _____ is defined as an obligation of an entity arising from past transactions or events, the settlement of which may result in the transfer or use of assets, provision of services or other yielding of economic benefits in the future.

a. False Claims Act
c. Vested
b. Corporate governance
d. Liability

35. The term _____ has a number of meanings in moral philosophy, in religion, and in layman's terms. Generally speaking, when someone says of an act that it is a '_____,' they refer to a belief that the act is one prescribed by their set of values.

Chapter 8. LONG-TERM OBLIGATIONS

Moral philosophers differ as to the origin of _____, and whether such obligations are external to the agent (that is, are, in some sense, objective and applicable to all agents) or are internal (that is, are based on the agent's personal desires, upbringing, conscience, and so on.)

    a. BNSF Railway
    b. BMC Software, Inc.
    c. Moral obligation
    d. 3M Company

36. The term _____ usually refers to a company that is permitted to offer its registered securities (stock, bonds, etc.) for sale to the general public, typically through a stock exchange, or occasionally a company whose stock is traded over the counter (OTC) via market makers who use non-exchange quotation services.

The term '_____' may also refer to a company owned by the government.

    a. Professional association
    b. MicroStrategy
    c. Governmental Accounting Standards Board
    d. Public Company

37. The _____ (sometimes called 'Peekaboo') is a private-sector, non-profit corporation created by the Sarbanes-Oxley Act, a 2002 United States federal law, to oversee the auditors of public companies. Its stated purpose is to 'protect the interests of investors and further the public interest in the preparation of informative, fair, and independent audit reports'. Although a private entity, the _____ has many government-like regulatory functions, making it in some ways similar to the private Self Regulatory Organizations (SROs) that regulate stock markets and other aspects of the financial markets in the United States.

    a. Pension Benefit Guaranty Corporation
    b. Financial Crimes Enforcement Network
    c. 3M Company
    d. Public Company Accounting Oversight Board

38. _____ of something is, in finance, the adding together of interest or different investments over a period of time such as atoms (1 - the act or process of accruing; 2 - the amount that accrues.) It holds specific meanings in accounting and payroll.

_____, in accounting, describes the accounting method known as _____ basis, whereby revenues and expenses are recognized when they are accrued, i.e. accumulated (earned or incurred), regardless when the actual cash is received or paid out.

    a. Accounts receivable
    b. Accrual
    c. Earnings before interest, taxes, depreciation and amortization
    d. Assets

39. _____ is a method of accounting whereby economic activities (rather than cash flow) of financial events are considered, because of two complementary principles, which (together) determine the point, at which expenses and revenues are recognized. According to revenue recognition principle, revenues are realized when earned, whether or not they are received in cash.

    a. Earnings before interest, taxes, depreciation and amortization
    b. Accrual basis accounting
    c. Accrued revenue
    d. Accrual

Chapter 8. LONG-TERM OBLIGATIONS

40. The _____ is a financial market where participants buy and sell debt securities, usually in the form of bonds. As of 2006, the size of the international _____ is an estimated $44.9 trillion, of which the size of the outstanding U.S. _____ debt was $25.2 trillion.

Nearly all of the $923 billion average daily trading volume in the U.S. _____ takes place between broker-dealers and large institutions in a decentralized, over-the-counter market.

   a. Demand curve
   b. Convertible bond
   c. Bond market
   d. Variance

41. _____ is a common concept in economics, and gives rise to derived concepts such as consumer debt. Generally _____ is defined by opposition to production. But the precise definition can vary because different schools of economists define production quite differently.
   a. Starving the beast
   b. Consumption
   c. Yield
   d. Mitigating Control

Chapter 9. BUSINESS-TYPE ACTIVITIES

1. The _____ is the national, professional association of CPAs in the United States, with more than 330,000 members, including CPAs in business and industry, public practice, government, and education; student affiliates; and international associates. It sets ethical standards for the profession and U.S. auditing standards for audits of private companies; federal, state and local governments; and non-profit organizations.

Approximately 40% of its members are engaged in the practice of public accounting, in areas such as auditing, accounting, taxation, general business consulting, business valuation, personal financial planning and business technology.

   a. AIG
   b. ABC Television Network
   c. Other postemployment benefits
   d. American Institute of Certified Public Accountants

2. Project _____: The project _____ is a prediction of the costs associated with a particular company project. These costs include labor, materials, and other related expenses. The project _____ is often broken down into specific tasks, with task _____s assigned to each.
   a. 3M Company
   b. BMC Software, Inc.
   c. Budget
   d. BNSF Railway

3. The _____ is a federal agency within the legislative branch of the United States government. It is a government agency that provides economic data to Congress. It was created by the Congressional Budget and Impoundment Control Act of 1974.
   a. 3M Company
   b. General Accounting Office
   c. BMC Software, Inc.
   d. Congressional Budget Office

4. The _____ is a private, not-for-profit organization whose primary purpose is to develop generally accepted accounting principles (GAAP) within the United States in the public's interest. The Securities and Exchange Commission (SEC) designated the _____ as the organization responsible for setting accounting standards for public companies in the U.S. It was created in 1973, replacing the Accounting Principles Board and the Committee on Accounting Procedure of the American Institute of Certified Public Accountants. The _____'s mission is 'to establish and improve standards of financial accounting and reporting for the guidance and education of the public, including issuers, auditors, and users of financial information.'

The _____ is not a governmental body.

   a. Financial Accounting Standards Board
   b. Public company
   c. Governmental Accounting Standards Board
   d. Fannie Mae

5. _____ is the term used to refer to the standard framework of guidelines for financial accounting used in any given jurisdiction. _____ includes the standards, conventions, and rules accountants follow in recording and summarizing transactions, and in the preparation of financial statements.

Financial accounting information must be assembled and reported objectively.

   a. General ledger
   b. Long-term liabilities
   c. Current asset
   d. Generally accepted accounting principles

Chapter 9. BUSINESS-TYPE ACTIVITIES

6. The _____ is currently the source of generally accepted accounting principles (GAAP) used by State and Local governments in the [[United States of America]]. As with most of the entities involved in creating GAAP in the United States, it is a private, non-governmental organization.

The _____ is subject to oversight by the Financial Accounting Foundation (FAF), which selects the members of the _____ and the Financial Accounting Standards Board, and funds both organizations.

a. Multinational corporation
b. Fannie Mae
c. National Conference of Commissioners on Uniform State Laws
d. Governmental Accounting Standards Board

7. The _____ was established as the _____ by the Budget and Accounting Act of 1921 (Pub.L. 67-13, 42 Stat. 20, June 10, 1921.)
a. BMC Software, Inc.
b. GAO
c. 3M Company
d. General Accounting Office

8. The _____ after Senator Harold Burton of Ohio and Senator Lister Hill of Alabama, is a United States federal law passed in 1946. This act responded to the first of Trumane;s proposals and was designed to provide federal grants and guaranteed loans to improve the physical plant of the natione;s hospital system. Money was designated to the states to achieve 4.5 beds per 1,000 people.
a. Model Code of Professional Responsibility
b. Tax patent
c. Lease
d. Hospital Survey and Construction Act

9. In finance, a _____ is a debt security, in which the authorized issuer owes the holders a debt and, depending on the terms of the _____, is obliged to pay interest (the coupon) and/or to repay the principal at a later date, termed maturity. It is a formal contract to repay borrowed money with interest at fixed intervals.

Thus a _____ is like a loan: the issuer is the borrower, the _____ holder is the lender, and the coupon is the interest.

a. Bond
b. Revenue bonds
c. Zero-coupon bond
d. Coupon rate

10. The word _____ indicates that a party, or proprietor, exercises private ownership, control or use over an item of property
a. Proprietary
b. 3M Company
c. BNSF Railway
d. BMC Software, Inc.

11. _____ are bonds issued by governments, authorities, or public benefit corporations that are guaranteed by the revenue flow of the issuing agency.

The Supreme Court decision of Pollock versus Farmer's Loan and Trust Company of 1895 initiated a wave or series of innovations for the financial services community in both tax-treatment and regulation from government. This specific case, according to a leading investment bank's research, resulted in the 'intergovernmental tax immunity doctrine,' ultimately leading to 'tax-free status.' Municipal bonds are generally exempt from federal tax on their interest payments (not capital gains.)

a. Municipal bond
b. Revenue bonds
c. Zero-coupon bond
d. Callable bond

12. _____ is the incidence or process of transferring ownership of a business, enterprise, agency or public service from the public sector (government) to the private sector (business.) In a broader sense, privatisation refers to transfer of any government function to the private sector including governmental functions like revenue collection and law enforcement.

The term 'Privatisation' also has been used to describe two unrelated transactions.

a. BMC Software, Inc.
b. Privatization
c. BNSF Railway
d. 3M Company

13. _____ is an accounting system often used by nonprofit organizations and by the public sector. According to StartHereGoPlaces, _____ is a '[m]ethod of accounting and presentation whereby assets and liabilities are grouped according to the purpose for which they are to be used.'

_____ serves any nonprofit organization or the public sector. These organizations have a need for special reporting to financial statements users that show how money is spent, rather than how much profit was earned.

a. Fund accounting
b. Replacement cost
c. Refunding
d. Liquidating dividend

14. _____ is a company's financial statement that indicates how the revenue is transformed into the net income The purpose of the _____ is to show managers and investors whether the company made or lost money during the period being reported.

The important thing to remember about an _____ is that it represents a period of time.

a. ABC Television Network
b. AIG
c. AMEX
d. Income statement

15. The _____ is located in Norwalk, Connecticut. It is an independent, organization in the private sector that is responsible for oversight of the Financial Accounting Standards Board (FASB), the Governmental Accounting Standards Board (GASB), and their respective advisory councils.

a. Financial Accounting Foundation
b. BMC Software, Inc.
c. BNSF Railway
d. 3M Company

16. An _____ is a term used in behavioral economics to describe those types of behaviors that impose costs on a person in the long-run that are not taken into account when making decisions in the present. Classical Economics discourages government from creating legislation that targets internalities, because it is assumed that the consumer takes these personal costs into account when paying for the good that causes the _____. For example, cigarettes should be taxed because of the negative consumption externalities that they impose, such as second-hand smoke, not because the smoker harms him or herself by smoking.

a. Operating budget
b. Authorised capital
c. Internality
d. Inventory turnover ratio

Chapter 9. BUSINESS-TYPE ACTIVITIES

17. In economics, _____ or _____ goods or real _____ refers to factors of production used to create goods or services that are not themselves significantly consumed (though they may depreciate) in the production process. _____ goods may be acquired with money or financial _____. In finance and accounting, _____ generally refers to financial wealth, especially that used to start or maintain a business.
    a. Vyborg Appeal
    b. Capital
    c. Screening
    d. Disclosure

18. The _____ duty is a legal relationship of confidence or trust between two or more parties, most commonly a _____ or trustee and a principal or beneficiary. One party, for example a corporate trust company or the trust department of a bank, holds a _____ relation or acts in a _____ capacity to another, such as one whose funds are entrusted to it for investment. In a _____ relation one person justifiably reposes confidence, good faith, reliance and trust in another whose aid, advice or protection is sought in some matter.
    a. FCPA
    b. Staple right
    c. Robinson-Patman Act
    d. Fiduciary

19. In business and accounting, _____ are everything of value that is owned by a person or company. It is a claim on the property your income of a borrower. The balance sheet of a firm records the monetary value of the _____ owned by the firm.
    a. Earnings before interest, taxes, depreciation and amortization
    b. Accrual basis accounting
    c. Assets
    d. Accounts receivable

20. _____ are securities that can be easily converted into cash. Such securities will generally have highly liquid markets allowing the security to be sold at a reasonable price very quickly. This is a usual feature in real estate .
    a. 3M Company
    b. Tracking stock
    c. BMC Software, Inc.
    d. Marketable

21. A _____ is a fungible, negotiable instrument representing financial value. they are broadly categorized into debt securities (such as banknotes, bonds and debentures), and equity securities; e.g., common stocks. The company or other entity issuing the _____ is called the issuer.
    a. BMC Software, Inc.
    b. 3M Company
    c. Tracking stock
    d. Security

22. In economics, business, retail, and accounting, a _____ is the value of money that has been used up to produce something, and hence is not available for use anymore. In economics, a _____ is an alternative that is given up as a result of a decision. In business, the _____ may be one of acquisition, in which case the amount of money expended to acquire it is counted as _____.
    a. Prime cost
    b. Cost allocation
    c. Cost of quality
    d. Cost

23. A _____ is a compensation, usually financial, received by a worker in exchange for their labor.

Compensation in terms of _____s is given to worker and compensation in terms of salary is given to employees. Compensation is a monetary benefits given to employees in returns of the services provided by them.

Chapter 9. BUSINESS-TYPE ACTIVITIES

a. Retirement plan
c. BMC Software, Inc.
b. 3M Company
d. Wage

24. The term _____ has three unrelated technical definitions, and is also used in a variety of non-technical ways.

- In financial economics, it refers to any asset used to make money, as opposed to assets used for personal enjoyment or consumption. This is an important distinction because two people can disagree sharply about the value of personal assets, one person might think a sports car is more valuable than a pickup truck, another person might have the opposite taste. But if an asset is held for the purpose of making money, taste has nothing to do with it, only differences of opinion about how much money the asset will produce. With the further assumption that people agree on the probability distribution of future cash flows, it is possible to have an objective _____ pricing model. Even without the assumption of agreement, it is possible to set rational limits on _____ value.
- In governmental accounting, it is defined as any asset used in operations with an initial useful life extending beyond one reporting period. Generally, government managers have a 'stewardship' duty to maintain _____ s under their control. See International Public Sector Accounting Standards for details.
- In US tax accounting, it is defined as any property other than a list of exceptions. The main exceptions are anything held for sale, and any real estate or depreciable property used in business. Almost everything you own and use for personal purposes, pleasure or investment is a _____. If something is a _____ for tax purposes, gains or losses on sale or disposition are capital gains or capital losses. For individuals, however, capital losses on property held for personal use are generally not deductible. See the IRS publication Tax Facts about Capital Gains and Losses for details.

A well-known financial accounting textbook advises that the term be avoided except in tax accounting because it is used in so many different senses, not all of them well-defined. For example it is often used as a synonym for fixed assets or for investments in securities.

A common non-technical usage occurs when people ask that employees or the environment or something else be treated as a _____.

a. 3M Company
c. Capital asset
b. BMC Software, Inc.
d. Solvency

25. The term _____ usually refers to a company that is permitted to offer its registered securities (stock, bonds, etc.) for sale to the general public, typically through a stock exchange, or occasionally a company whose stock is traded over the counter (OTC) via market makers who use non-exchange quotation services.

The term '_____' may also refer to a company owned by the government.

a. Governmental Accounting Standards Board
c. Professional association
b. MicroStrategy
d. Public Company

Chapter 9. BUSINESS-TYPE ACTIVITIES

26. The _____ (sometimes called 'Peekaboo') is a private-sector, non-profit corporation created by the Sarbanes-Oxley Act, a 2002 United States federal law, to oversee the auditors of public companies. Its stated purpose is to 'protect the interests of investors and further the public interest in the preparation of informative, fair, and independent audit reports'. Although a private entity, the _____ has many government-like regulatory functions, making it in some ways similar to the private Self Regulatory Organizations (SROs) that regulate stock markets and other aspects of the financial markets in the United States.
    a. Pension Benefit Guaranty Corporation
    b. Financial Crimes Enforcement Network
    c. 3M Company
    d. Public Company Accounting Oversight Board

27. A budget _____ occurs when an entity spends more money than it takes in. The opposite of a budget _____ is a budget surplus. Debt is essentially an accumulated flow of _____s.
    a. Deficit
    b. Windfall profits tax
    c. Land value taxation
    d. Progressive tax

28. _____ is a risk management method in which a calculated amount of money is set aside to compensate for the potential future loss.

If _____ is approached as a serious risk management technique, money is set aside using actuarial and insurance information and the law of large numbers so that the amount set aside (similar to an insurance premium) is enough to cover the future uncertain loss.

_____ is possible for any insurable risk, meaning a risk that is predictable and measurable enough in the aggregate to be able to estimate the amount that needs to be set aside to pay for future uncertain losses.

   a. Self insurance
   b. 3M Company
   c. Loss ratio
   d. BMC Software, Inc.

29. _____ is that which is owed; usually referencing assets owed, but the term can also cover moral obligations and other interactions not requiring money. In the case of assets, _____ is a means of using future purchasing power in the present before a summation has been earned. Some companies and corporations use _____ as a part of their overall corporate finance strategy.
    a. Lender
    b. Loan
    c. Debenture
    d. Debt

30. _____ in the United States currently refers to the federal Old-Age, Survivors, and Disability Insurance (OASDI) program.

Chapter 9. BUSINESS-TYPE ACTIVITIES

The original _____ Act and the current version of the Act, as amended encompass several social welfare and social insurance programs. The larger and better known programs are:

- Federal Old-Age, Survivors, and Disability Insurance
- Unemployment benefits
- Temporary Assistance for Needy Families
- Health Insurance for Aged and Disabled (Medicare)
- Grants to States for Medical Assistance Programs (Medicaid)
- State Children's Health Insurance Program (SCHIP)
- Supplemental Security Income (Social Securityl)

U.S. _____ is a social insurance program funded through dedicated payroll taxes called Federal Insurance Contributions Act (FICA.) Tax deposits are formally entrusted to Federal Old-Age and Survivors Insurance Trust Fund, or Federal Disability Insurance Trust Fund, Federal Hospital Insurance Trust Fund or the Federal Supplementary Medical Insurance Trust Fund.

a. Sale
b. Social Security
c. Comparable
d. Price-to-sales ratio

31. The United States _____ is an independent agency of the United States federal government that administers Social Security, a social insurance program consisting of retirement, disability, and survivors' benefits. To qualify for these benefits, most American workers pay Social Security taxes on their earnings; future benefits are based on the employees' contributions.

The _____ was established by a law currently codified at 42 U.S.C.

a. Social Security Administration
b. Return on assets
c. Minority interest
d. Time value of money

32. _____ is a common concept in economics, and gives rise to derived concepts such as consumer debt. Generally _____ is defined by opposition to production. But the precise definition can vary because different schools of economists define production quite differently.

a. Mitigating Control
b. Yield
c. Starving the beast
d. Consumption

Chapter 10. FIDUCIARY FUNDS AND PERMANENT FUNDS

1. The _____ is the national, professional association of CPAs in the United States, with more than 330,000 members, including CPAs in business and industry, public practice, government, and education; student affiliates; and international associates. It sets ethical standards for the profession and U.S. auditing standards for audits of private companies; federal, state and local governments; and non-profit organizations.

Approximately 40% of its members are engaged in the practice of public accounting, in areas such as auditing, accounting, taxation, general business consulting, business valuation, personal financial planning and business technology.

   a. AIG
   b. American Institute of Certified Public Accountants
   c. Other postemployment benefits
   d. ABC Television Network

2. The _____ is currently the source of generally accepted accounting principles (GAAP) used by State and Local governments in the [[United States of America]]. As with most of the entities involved in creating GAAP in the United States, it is a private, non-governmental organization.

The _____ is subject to oversight by the Financial Accounting Foundation (FAF), which selects the members of the _____ and the Financial Accounting Standards Board, and funds both organizations.

   a. National Conference of Commissioners on Uniform State Laws
   b. Fannie Mae
   c. Multinational corporation
   d. Governmental Accounting Standards Board

3. In business and accounting, _____ are everything of value that is owned by a person or company. It is a claim on the property your income of a borrower. The balance sheet of a firm records the monetary value of the _____ owned by the firm.
   a. Accounts receivable
   b. Accrual basis accounting
   c. Earnings before interest, taxes, depreciation and amortization
   d. Assets

4. Project _____: The project _____ is a prediction of the costs associated with a particular company project. These costs include labor, materials, and other related expenses. The project _____ is often broken down into specific tasks, with task _____s assigned to each.
   a. BNSF Railway
   b. 3M Company
   c. BMC Software, Inc.
   d. Budget

5. The _____ duty is a legal relationship of confidence or trust between two or more parties, most commonly a _____ or trustee and a principal or beneficiary. One party, for example a corporate trust company or the trust department of a bank, holds a _____ relation or acts in a _____ capacity to another, such as one whose funds are entrusted to it for investment. In a _____ relation one person justifiably reposes confidence, good faith, reliance and trust in another whose aid, advice or protection is sought in some matter.
   a. Robinson-Patman Act
   b. Staple right
   c. FCPA
   d. Fiduciary

6. _____ are formal records of a business' financial activities.

Chapter 10. FIDUCIARY FUNDS AND PERMANENT FUNDS 71

In British English, including United Kingdom company law, _____ are often referred to as accounts, although the term _____ is also used, particularly by accountants.

_____ provide an overview of a business' financial condition in both short and long term.

  a. Financial statements
  c. 3M Company
  b. Notes to the financial statements
  d. Statement of retained earnings

7. To tax is to impose a financial charge or other levy upon a _____ by a state or the functional equivalent of a state.

Taxes are also imposed by many subnational entities. Taxes consist of direct tax or indirect tax, and may be paid in money or as its labour equivalent (often but not always unpaid.)

  a. Tax avoidance
  c. State tax levels
  b. Taxpayer
  d. Federal Unemployment Tax Act

8. _____ is a specific term used in companies' financial reporting from the company-whole point of view. Because that use excludes the effects of changing ownership interest, an economic measure of _____ is necessary for financial analysis from the shareholders' point of view

_____ is defined by the Financial Accounting Standards Board, or FASB, as 'the change in equity [net assets] of a business enterprise during a period from transactions and other events and circumstances from nonowner sources. It includes all changes in equity during a period except those resulting from investments by owners and distributions to owners.'

_____ is the sum of net income and other items that must bypass the income statement because they have not been realized, including items like an unrealized holding gain or loss from available for sale securities and foreign currency translation gains or losses.

  a. 3M Company
  c. BNSF Railway
  b. BMC Software, Inc.
  d. Comprehensive income

9. The _____ is a federal agency within the legislative branch of the United States government. It is a government agency that provides economic data to Congress. It was created by the Congressional Budget and Impoundment Control Act of 1974.
  a. General Accounting Office
  c. BMC Software, Inc.
  b. 3M Company
  d. Congressional Budget Office

Chapter 10. FIDUCIARY FUNDS AND PERMANENT FUNDS

10. The _____ is a private, not-for-profit organization whose primary purpose is to develop generally accepted accounting principles (GAAP) within the United States in the public's interest. The Securities and Exchange Commission (SEC) designated the _____ as the organization responsible for setting accounting standards for public companies in the U.S. It was created in 1973, replacing the Accounting Principles Board and the Committee on Accounting Procedure of the American Institute of Certified Public Accountants. The _____'s mission is 'to establish and improve standards of financial accounting and reporting for the guidance and education of the public, including issuers, auditors, and users of financial information.'

The _____ is not a governmental body.

  a. Governmental Accounting Standards Board
  b. Public company
  c. Fannie Mae
  d. Financial Accounting Standards Board

11. _____ is the term used to refer to the standard framework of guidelines for financial accounting used in any given jurisdiction. _____ includes the standards, conventions, and rules accountants follow in recording and summarizing transactions, and in the preparation of financial statements.

Financial accounting information must be assembled and reported objectively.

  a. Long-term liabilities
  b. Current asset
  c. Generally accepted accounting principles
  d. General ledger

12. _____ is a term used in accounting, economics and finance to spread the cost of an asset over the span of several years.

In simple words we can say that _____ is the reduction in the value of an asset due to usage, passage of time, wear and tear, technological outdating or obsolescence, depletion, inadequacy, rot, rust, decay or other such factors.

In accounting, _____ is a term used to describe any method of attributing the historical or purchase cost of an asset across its useful life, roughly corresponding to normal wear and tear.

  a. Current asset
  b. Depreciation
  c. General ledger
  d. Net profit

13. _____ is an accounting system often used by nonprofit organizations and by the public sector. According to StartHereGoPlaces, _____ is a '[m]ethod of accounting and presentation whereby assets and liabilities are grouped according to the purpose for which they are to be used.'

_____ serves any nonprofit organization or the public sector. These organizations have a need for special reporting to financial statements users that show how money is spent, rather than how much profit was earned.

  a. Fund accounting
  b. Replacement cost
  c. Liquidating dividend
  d. Refunding

Chapter 10. FIDUCIARY FUNDS AND PERMANENT FUNDS

14. An _____ is a practitioner of accountancy, which is the measurement, disclosure or provision of assurance about financial information that helps managers, investors, tax authorities and other decision makers make resource allocation decisions.

The word '_____' is derived from the French 'Compter' which took its origin from the Latin 'Computare'. The word was formerly written in English as 'Accomptant', but in process of time the word, which was always pronounced by dropping the 'p', became gradually changed both in pronunciation and in orthography to its present form.

   a. ABC Television Network   b. Accountant
   c. AMEX   d. AIG

15. The _____ is the global organization for the accountancy profession. IFAC has 157 member bodies and associates in 123 countries and jurisdictions, representing more than 2.5 million accountants employed in public practice, industry and commerce, government, and academe. The organization, through its independent standard-setting boards, establishes international standards on ethics, auditing and assurance, education, and public sector accounting.

   a. International Accounting Standards Committee   b. American Payroll Association
   c. Emerging technologies   d. International Federation of Accountants

16. The _____ after Senator Harold Burton of Ohio and Senator Lister Hill of Alabama, is a United States federal law passed in 1946. This act responded to the first of Trumane;s proposals and was designed to provide federal grants and guaranteed loans to improve the physical plant of the natione;s hospital system. Money was designated to the states to achieve 4.5 beds per 1,000 people.

   a. Model Code of Professional Responsibility   b. Lease
   c. Tax patent   d. Hospital Survey and Construction Act

17. In economics, _____ is a rise in the general level of prices of goods and services in an economy over a period of time. When the general price level rises, each unit of currency buys fewer goods and services; consequently, _____ is also a decline in the real value of money--a loss of purchasing power in the medium of exchange which is also the monetary unit of account in the economy. A chief measure of general price-level _____ is the general _____ rate, which is the percentage change in a general price index (normally the Consumer Price Index) over time.

   a. Opportunity cost   b. ABC Television Network
   c. AIG   d. Inflation

18. The _____ is a Cabinet-level office, and is the largest office within the Executive Office of the President of the United States (EOP.) It is an important conduit by which the White House oversees the activities of federal agencies. OMB is tasked with giving expert advice to senior White House officials on a range of topics relating to federal policy, management, legislative, regulatory, and budgetary issues.

   a. Analysis of variance   b. Office of Management and Budget
   c. Alaska Air Group   d. AT'T Wireless Services, Inc.

19. A _____ is a pool of assets forming an independent legal entity that are bought with the contributions to a pension plan for the exclusive purpose of financing pension plan benefits.

_____s are important shareholders of listed and private companies. They are especially important to the stock market where large institutional investors like the Ontario Teachers' Pension Plan dominate.

Chapter 10. FIDUCIARY FUNDS AND PERMANENT FUNDS

a. Public offering
b. Return on assets
c. Limited liability company
d. Pension fund

20. In economics, business, retail, and accounting, a _____ is the value of money that has been used up to produce something, and hence is not available for use anymore. In economics, a _____ is an alternative that is given up as a result of a decision. In business, the _____ may be one of acquisition, in which case the amount of money expended to acquire it is counted as _____.

a. Cost of quality
b. Cost allocation
c. Prime cost
d. Cost

21. A _____ is a compensation, usually financial, received by a worker in exchange for their labor.

Compensation in terms of _____s is given to worker and compensation in terms of salary is given to employees. Compensation is a monetary benefits given to employees in returns of the services provided by them.

a. Wage
b. Retirement plan
c. BMC Software, Inc.
d. 3M Company

22. The term _____ usually refers to a company that is permitted to offer its registered securities (stock, bonds, etc.) for sale to the general public, typically through a stock exchange, or occasionally a company whose stock is traded over the counter (OTC) via market makers who use non-exchange quotation services.

The term '_____' may also refer to a company owned by the government.

a. Governmental Accounting Standards Board
b. Professional association
c. MicroStrategy
d. Public Company

23. The _____ (sometimes called 'Peekaboo') is a private-sector, non-profit corporation created by the Sarbanes-Oxley Act, a 2002 United States federal law, to oversee the auditors of public companies. Its stated purpose is to 'protect the interests of investors and further the public interest in the preparation of informative, fair, and independent audit reports'. Although a private entity, the _____ has many government-like regulatory functions, making it in some ways similar to the private Self Regulatory Organizations (SROs) that regulate stock markets and other aspects of the financial markets in the United States.

a. 3M Company
b. Pension Benefit Guaranty Corporation
c. Public Company Accounting Oversight Board
d. Financial Crimes Enforcement Network

24. An _____ is a company whose main business is holding securities of other companies purely for investment purposes. The _____ invests money on behalf of its shareholders who in turn share in the profits and losses.

In United States securities law, there are at least three types of investment companies :

- Open-End Management Investment Companies (mutual funds)
- Closed-End Management Investment Companies (closed-end funds)
- UITs (unit investment trusts)

Chapter 10. FIDUCIARY FUNDS AND PERMANENT FUNDS

A fourth and lesser-known type of _____ under the _____ Act of 1940 is a Face-Amount Certificate Company.

   a. AMEX
   c. AIG
   b. ABC Television Network
   d. Investment Company

25. The _____ is an act of Congress. It was passed as a United States Public Law (PL-768) on August 22, 1940, and is codified at 15 U.S.C. §§ 80a-1 through 15 U.S.C.

   a. ABC Television Network
   c. AMEX
   b. Investment Company Act of 1940
   d. AIG

Chapter 11. ISSUES OF REPORTING, DISCLOSURE, AND FINANCIAL ANALYSIS

1. Project _____: The project _____ is a prediction of the costs associated with a particular company project. These costs include labor, materials, and other related expenses. The project _____ is often broken down into specific tasks, with task _____s assigned to each.
   a. BMC Software, Inc.
   b. BNSF Railway
   c. 3M Company
   d. Budget

2. The _____ is a federal agency within the legislative branch of the United States government. It is a government agency that provides economic data to Congress. It was created by the Congressional Budget and Impoundment Control Act of 1974.
   a. General Accounting Office
   b. BMC Software, Inc.
   c. 3M Company
   d. Congressional Budget Office

3. The _____ is currently the source of generally accepted accounting principles (GAAP) used by State and Local governments in the [[United States of America]]. As with most of the entities involved in creating GAAP in the United States, it is a private, non-governmental organization.

   The _____ is subject to oversight by the Financial Accounting Foundation (FAF), which selects the members of the _____ and the Financial Accounting Standards Board, and funds both organizations.

   a. Fannie Mae
   b. National Conference of Commissioners on Uniform State Laws
   c. Multinational corporation
   d. Governmental Accounting Standards Board

4. A _____ is a fungible, negotiable instrument representing financial value. they are broadly categorized into debt securities (such as banknotes, bonds and debentures), and equity securities; e.g., common stocks. The company or other entity issuing the _____ is called the issuer.
   a. Security
   b. BMC Software, Inc.
   c. 3M Company
   d. Tracking stock

5. _____ in the United States currently refers to the federal Old-Age, Survivors, and Disability Insurance (OASDI) program.

   The original _____ Act and the current version of the Act, as amended encompass several social welfare and social insurance programs. The larger and better known programs are:

   - Federal Old-Age, Survivors, and Disability Insurance
   - Unemployment benefits
   - Temporary Assistance for Needy Families
   - Health Insurance for Aged and Disabled (Medicare)
   - Grants to States for Medical Assistance Programs (Medicaid)
   - State Children's Health Insurance Program (SCHIP)
   - Supplemental Security Income (Social Securityl)

   U.S. _____ is a social insurance program funded through dedicated payroll taxes called Federal Insurance Contributions Act (FICA.) Tax deposits are formally entrusted to Federal Old-Age and Survivors Insurance Trust Fund, or Federal Disability Insurance Trust Fund, Federal Hospital Insurance Trust Fund or the Federal Supplementary Medical Insurance Trust Fund.

Chapter 11. ISSUES OF REPORTING, DISCLOSURE, AND FINANCIAL ANALYSIS 77

a. Sale
b. Price-to-sales ratio
c. Comparable
d. Social Security

6. The United States _____ is an independent agency of the United States federal government that administers Social Security, a social insurance program consisting of retirement, disability, and survivors' benefits. To qualify for these benefits, most American workers pay Social Security taxes on their earnings; future benefits are based on the employees' contributions.

The _____ was established by a law currently codified at 42 U.S.C.

a. Time value of money
b. Minority interest
c. Return on assets
d. Social Security Administration

7. _____ is concerned with the provisions and use of accounting information to managers within organizations, to provide them with the basis to make informed business decisions that will allow them to be better equipped in their management and control functions.

In contrast to financial accountancy information, _____ information is:

- usually confidential and used by management, instead of publicly reported;
- forward-looking, instead of historical;
- pragmatically computed using extensive management information systems and internal controls, instead of complying with accounting standards.

This is because of the different emphasis: _____ information is used within an organization, typically for decision-making.

a. Nonassurance services
b. Governmental accounting
c. Grenzplankostenrechnung
d. Management accounting

8. The _____ is the national, professional association of CPAs in the United States, with more than 330,000 members, including CPAs in business and industry, public practice, government, and education; student affiliates; and international associates. It sets ethical standards for the profession and U.S. auditing standards for audits of private companies; federal, state and local governments; and non-profit organizations.

Approximately 40% of its members are engaged in the practice of public accounting, in areas such as auditing, accounting, taxation, general business consulting, business valuation, personal financial planning and business technology.

a. ABC Television Network
b. Other postemployment benefits
c. AIG
d. American Institute of Certified Public Accountants

9. A _____ is an administrative entity composed of a clearly defined territory and its population and commonly denotes a city, town or a small grouping of them. A _____ is typically governed by a mayor and a city council or municipal council.

Chapter 11. ISSUES OF REPORTING, DISCLOSURE, AND FINANCIAL ANALYSIS

The notion of _____ includes townships but is not restricted to them.

a. BMC Software, Inc.
c. 3M Company
b. BNSF Railway
d. Municipality

10. The _____ of a company or public agency is the corporate officer primarily responsible for managing the financial risks of the business or agency. This officer is also responsible for financial planning and record-keeping, as well as financial reporting to higher management. (In recent years, however, the role has expanded to encompass communicating financial performance and forecasts to the analyst community.)

a. Merck ' Co., Inc.
c. NASDAQ
b. Chief executive officer
d. Chief Financial Officer

11. The _____ signed into law by President George H.W. Bush on November 15, 1990, is a United States federal law intended to improve the government's financial management, outlining standards of financial performance and disclosure. Among other measures, the Office of Management and Budget (OMB) was given greater authority over federal financial management. For each of 23 federal departments and agencies, the position of chief financial officer was created.

a. Scottish Poor Laws
c. Jenkins Committee
b. Bylaw
d. Chief Financial Officers Act of 1990

12. _____ is the term used to refer to the standard framework of guidelines for financial accounting used in any given jurisdiction. _____ includes the standards, conventions, and rules accountants follow in recording and summarizing transactions, and in the preparation of financial statements.

Financial accounting information must be assembled and reported objectively.

a. Current asset
c. General ledger
b. Generally accepted accounting principles
d. Long-term liabilities

13. The term _____ refers to government debt, expenditures and revenues, or to finance (particularly financial revenue) in general.

- _____ deficit is the budget deficit of federal or local government
- _____ policy is the discretionary spending of governments. Contrasts with monetary policy.
- _____ year and _____ quarter are reporting periods for firms and other agencies.

See also

- Procurator _____ and Crown Office and Procurator _____ Service

a. Swap
c. Fiscal
b. Comparable
d. Scientific Research and Experimental Development Tax Incentive Program

Chapter 11. ISSUES OF REPORTING, DISCLOSURE, AND FINANCIAL ANALYSIS

14. The _____ after Senator Harold Burton of Ohio and Senator Lister Hill of Alabama, is a United States federal law passed in 1946. This act responded to the first of Trumane;s proposals and was designed to provide federal grants and guaranteed loans to improve the physical plant of the natione;s hospital system. Money was designated to the states to achieve 4.5 beds per 1,000 people.
    a. Model Code of Professional Responsibility
    b. Lease
    c. Tax patent
    d. Hospital Survey and Construction Act

15. The _____ was established as the _____ by the Budget and Accounting Act of 1921 (Pub.L. 67-13, 42 Stat. 20, June 10, 1921.)
    a. 3M Company
    b. General Accounting Office
    c. BMC Software, Inc.
    d. GAO

16. The term _____ usually refers to a company that is permitted to offer its registered securities (stock, bonds, etc.) for sale to the general public, typically through a stock exchange, or occasionally a company whose stock is traded over the counter (OTC) via market makers who use non-exchange quotation services.

The term '_____' may also refer to a company owned by the government.

    a. Professional association
    b. Public Company
    c. MicroStrategy
    d. Governmental Accounting Standards Board

17. The _____ (sometimes called 'Peekaboo') is a private-sector, non-profit corporation created by the Sarbanes-Oxley Act, a 2002 United States federal law, to oversee the auditors of public companies. Its stated purpose is to 'protect the interests of investors and further the public interest in the preparation of informative, fair, and independent audit reports'. Although a private entity, the _____ has many government-like regulatory functions, making it in some ways similar to the private Self Regulatory Organizations (SROs) that regulate stock markets and other aspects of the financial markets in the United States.
    a. Financial Crimes Enforcement Network
    b. 3M Company
    c. Public Company Accounting Oversight Board
    d. Pension Benefit Guaranty Corporation

18. A budget _____ occurs when an entity spends more money than it takes in. The opposite of a budget _____ is a budget surplus. Debt is essentially an accumulated flow of _____s.
    a. Windfall profits tax
    b. Land value taxation
    c. Progressive tax
    d. Deficit

19. In financial accounting, a _____ is defined as an obligation of an entity arising from past transactions or events, the settlement of which may result in the transfer or use of assets, provision of services or other yielding of economic benefits in the future.
    a. Corporate governance
    b. False Claims Act
    c. Vested
    d. Liability

Chapter 12. OTHER NOT-FOR-PROFIT ORGANIZATIONS

1. The _____ is the national, professional association of CPAs in the United States, with more than 330,000 members, including CPAs in business and industry, public practice, government, and education; student affiliates; and international associates. It sets ethical standards for the profession and U.S. auditing standards for audits of private companies; federal, state and local governments; and non-profit organizations.

Approximately 40% of its members are engaged in the practice of public accounting, in areas such as auditing, accounting, taxation, general business consulting, business valuation, personal financial planning and business technology.

   a. Other postemployment benefits
   b. AIG
   c. American Institute of Certified Public Accountants
   d. ABC Television Network

2. The _____ is a private, not-for-profit organization whose primary purpose is to develop generally accepted accounting principles (GAAP) within the United States in the public's interest. The Securities and Exchange Commission (SEC) designated the _____ as the organization responsible for setting accounting standards for public companies in the U.S. It was created in 1973, replacing the Accounting Principles Board and the Committee on Accounting Procedure of the American Institute of Certified Public Accountants. The _____'s mission is 'to establish and improve standards of financial accounting and reporting for the guidance and education of the public, including issuers, auditors, and users of financial information.'

The _____ is not a governmental body.

   a. Governmental Accounting Standards Board
   b. Fannie Mae
   c. Public company
   d. Financial Accounting Standards Board

3. The _____ was established as the _____ by the Budget and Accounting Act of 1921 (Pub.L. 67-13, 42 Stat. 20, June 10, 1921.)
   a. 3M Company
   b. GAO
   c. BMC Software, Inc.
   d. General Accounting Office

4. Project _____: The project _____ is a prediction of the costs associated with a particular company project. These costs include labor, materials, and other related expenses. The project _____ is often broken down into specific tasks, with task _____s assigned to each.
   a. BMC Software, Inc.
   b. Budget
   c. 3M Company
   d. BNSF Railway

5. The _____ is a federal agency within the legislative branch of the United States government. It is a government agency that provides economic data to Congress. It was created by the Congressional Budget and Impoundment Control Act of 1974.
   a. 3M Company
   b. General Accounting Office
   c. BMC Software, Inc.
   d. Congressional Budget Office

6. _____ is the term used to refer to the standard framework of guidelines for financial accounting used in any given jurisdiction. _____ includes the standards, conventions, and rules accountants follow in recording and summarizing transactions, and in the preparation of financial statements.

Financial accounting information must be assembled and reported objectively.

Chapter 12. OTHER NOT-FOR-PROFIT ORGANIZATIONS

a. Current asset
c. General ledger
b. Generally accepted accounting principles
d. Long-term liabilities

7. The term _____ usually refers to a company that is permitted to offer its registered securities (stock, bonds, etc.) for sale to the general public, typically through a stock exchange, or occasionally a company whose stock is traded over the counter (OTC) via market makers who use non-exchange quotation services.

The term '_____' may also refer to a company owned by the government.

a. Governmental Accounting Standards Board
c. MicroStrategy
b. Professional association
d. Public Company

8. The _____ (sometimes called 'Peekaboo') is a private-sector, non-profit corporation created by the Sarbanes-Oxley Act, a 2002 United States federal law, to oversee the auditors of public companies. Its stated purpose is to 'protect the interests of investors and further the public interest in the preparation of informative, fair, and independent audit reports'. Although a private entity, the _____ has many government-like regulatory functions, making it in some ways similar to the private Self Regulatory Organizations (SROs) that regulate stock markets and other aspects of the financial markets in the United States.

a. Pension Benefit Guaranty Corporation
c. Financial Crimes Enforcement Network
b. 3M Company
d. Public Company Accounting Oversight Board

9. The term _____ is used in finance theory to refer to any terminating stream of fixed payments over a specified period of time. This usage is most commonly seen in academic discussions of finance, usually in connection with the valuation of the stream of payments, taking into account time value of money concepts such as interest rate and future value.

Examples of these are regular deposits to a savings account, monthly home mortgage payments and monthly insurance payments.

a. Intangible
c. Appropriation
b. Improvement
d. Annuity

10. In business and accounting, _____ are everything of value that is owned by a person or company. It is a claim on the property your income of a borrower. The balance sheet of a firm records the monetary value of the _____ owned by the firm.

a. Earnings before interest, taxes, depreciation and amortization
c. Assets
b. Accounts receivable
d. Accrual basis accounting

11. _____ are formal records of a business' financial activities.

In British English, including United Kingdom company law, _____ are often referred to as accounts, although the term _____ is also used, particularly by accountants.

_____ provide an overview of a business' financial condition in both short and long term.

a. Notes to the financial statements
c. 3M Company
b. Statement of retained earnings
d. Financial statements

12. In financial accounting, a _____ or statement of financial position is a summary of a person's or organization's balances. Assets, liabilities and ownership equity are listed as of a specific date, such as the end of its financial year. A _____ is often described as a snapshot of a company's financial condition.
   a. Financial statements
   b. 3M Company
   c. Statement of retained earnings
   d. Balance sheet

13. A _____ is a fungible, negotiable instrument representing financial value. they are broadly categorized into debt securities (such as banknotes, bonds and debentures), and equity securities; e.g., common stocks. The company or other entity issuing the _____ is called the issuer.
   a. BMC Software, Inc.
   b. Tracking stock
   c. Security
   d. 3M Company

14. _____ in the United States currently refers to the federal Old-Age, Survivors, and Disability Insurance (OASDI) program.

The original _____ Act and the current version of the Act, as amended encompass several social welfare and social insurance programs. The larger and better known programs are:

- Federal Old-Age, Survivors, and Disability Insurance
- Unemployment benefits
- Temporary Assistance for Needy Families
- Health Insurance for Aged and Disabled (Medicare)
- Grants to States for Medical Assistance Programs (Medicaid)
- State Children's Health Insurance Program (SCHIP)
- Supplemental Security Income (Social Securityl)

U.S. _____ is a social insurance program funded through dedicated payroll taxes called Federal Insurance Contributions Act (FICA.) Tax deposits are formally entrusted to Federal Old-Age and Survivors Insurance Trust Fund, or Federal Disability Insurance Trust Fund, Federal Hospital Insurance Trust Fund or the Federal Supplementary Medical Insurance Trust Fund.

   a. Comparable
   b. Sale
   c. Price-to-sales ratio
   d. Social Security

15. The United States _____ is an independent agency of the United States federal government that administers Social Security, a social insurance program consisting of retirement, disability, and survivors' benefits. To qualify for these benefits, most American workers pay Social Security taxes on their earnings; future benefits are based on the employees' contributions.

The _____ was established by a law currently codified at 42 U.S.C.

Chapter 12. OTHER NOT-FOR-PROFIT ORGANIZATIONS

a. Minority interest
c. Return on assets
b. Time value of money
d. Social Security Administration

16. In accounting, _____ has a very specific meaning. It is an outflow of cash or other valuable assets from a person or company to another person or company. This outflow of cash is generally one side of a trade for products or services that have equal or better current or future value to the buyer than to the seller.
    a. AMEX
    c. ABC Television Network
    b. AIG
    d. Expense

17. The _____ is currently the source of generally accepted accounting principles (GAAP) used by State and Local governments in the [[United States of America]]. As with most of the entities involved in creating GAAP in the United States, it is a private, non-governmental organization.

The _____ is subject to oversight by the Financial Accounting Foundation (FAF), which selects the members of the _____ and the Financial Accounting Standards Board, and funds both organizations.

a. National Conference of Commissioners on Uniform State Laws
c. Fannie Mae
b. Governmental Accounting Standards Board
d. Multinational corporation

18. _____ is the balance of the amounts of cash being received and paid by a business during a defined period of time, sometimes tied to a specific project. Measurement of _____ can be used

- to evaluate the state or performance of a business or project.
- to determine problems with liquidity. Being profitable does not necessarily mean being liquid. A company can fail because of a shortage of cash, even while profitable.
- to project rate of returns. The time of _____s into and out of projects are used as inputs to financial models such as internal rate of return, and net present value.
- to examine income or growth of a business when it is believed that accrual accounting concepts do not represent economic realities. Alternately, _____ can be used to 'validate' the net income generated by accrual accounting.

_____ as a generic term may be used differently depending on context, and certain _____ definitions may be adapted by analysts and users for their own uses. Common terms include operating _____ and free _____.

a. Flow-through entity
c. Commercial paper
b. Controlling interest
d. Cash flow

19. _____ are payments made by a corporation to its shareholder members. It is the portion of corporate profits paid out to stockholders. When a corporation earns a profit or surplus, that money can be put to two uses: it can either be re-invested in the business (called retained earnings), or it can be paid to the shareholders as a dividend.
    a. Dividends
    c. Dividend yield
    b. Dividend payout ratio
    d. Dividend stripping

Chapter 12. OTHER NOT-FOR-PROFIT ORGANIZATIONS

20. The _____ after Senator Harold Burton of Ohio and Senator Lister Hill of Alabama, is a United States federal law passed in 1946. This act responded to the first of Trumane;s proposals and was designed to provide federal grants and guaranteed loans to improve the physical plant of the natione;s hospital system. Money was designated to the states to achieve 4.5 beds per 1,000 people.

a. Tax patent
b. Model Code of Professional Responsibility
c. Lease
d. Hospital Survey and Construction Act

21. The _____ of a company or public agency is the corporate officer primarily responsible for managing the financial risks of the business or agency. This officer is also responsible for financial planning and record-keeping, as well as financial reporting to higher management. (In recent years, however, the role has expanded to encompass communicating financial performance and forecasts to the analyst community.)

a. Chief executive officer
b. NASDAQ
c. Merck ' Co., Inc.
d. Chief Financial Officer

22. The _____ signed into law by President George H.W. Bush on November 15, 1990, is a United States federal law intended to improve the government's financial management, outlining standards of financial performance and disclosure. Among other measures, the Office of Management and Budget (OMB) was given greater authority over federal financial management. For each of 23 federal departments and agencies, the position of chief financial officer was created.

a. Bylaw
b. Jenkins Committee
c. Scottish Poor Laws
d. Chief Financial Officers Act of 1990

23. The _____ is a Cabinet-level office, and is the largest office within the Executive Office of the President of the United States (EOP.) It is an important conduit by which the White House oversees the activities of federal agencies. OMB is tasked with giving expert advice to senior White House officials on a range of topics relating to federal policy, management, legislative, regulatory, and budgetary issues.

a. Analysis of variance
b. Alaska Air Group
c. AT'T Wireless Services, Inc.
d. Office of Management and Budget

24. An _____ is a practitioner of accountancy, which is the measurement, disclosure or provision of assurance about financial information that helps managers, investors, tax authorities and other decision makers make resource allocation decisions.

The word '_____' is derived from the French 'Compter' which took its origin from the Latin 'Computare'. The word was formerly written in English as 'Accomptant', but in process of time the word, which was always pronounced by dropping the 'p', became gradually changed both in pronunciation and in orthography to its present form.

a. AIG
b. AMEX
c. ABC Television Network
d. Accountant

25. The _____ is the global organization for the accountancy profession. IFAC has 157 member bodies and associates in 123 countries and jurisdictions, representing more than 2.5 million accountants employed in public practice, industry and commerce, government, and academe. The organization, through its independent standard-setting boards, establishes international standards on ethics,auditing and assurance, education, and public sector accounting.

Chapter 12. OTHER NOT-FOR-PROFIT ORGANIZATIONS 85

a. International Federation of Accountants
b. American Payroll Association
c. Emerging technologies
d. International Accounting Standards Committee

26. In the United States, _____ federal benefits is defined as any federal program, project, service, and activity provided by the federal government that directly assists or benefits the American public in the areas of education, health, public safety, public welfare, and public works, among others. The assistance, which can reach to over $400 billion dollars annually, is provided and administered by federal government agencies, such as the U.S. Department of Housing and Urban Development and the U.S. Department of Health and Human Services, through special programs to recipients.

The term assistance is defined by the federal government as:

In order to provide _____ in an organized manner, the federal government provides assistance through federal agencies.

a. Federal assistance
b. BNSF Railway
c. 3M Company
d. BMC Software, Inc.

27. _____ is a fee paid on borrowed assets. It is the price paid for the use of borrowed money, or, money earned by deposited funds. Assets that are sometimes lent with _____ include money, shares, consumer goods through hire purchase, major assets such as aircraft, and even entire factories in finance lease arrangements. The _____ is calculated upon the value of the assets in the same manner as upon money.

a. Interest
b. ABC Television Network
c. AIG
d. Insolvency

28. To tax is to impose a financial charge or other levy upon a _____ by a state or the functional equivalent of a state.

Taxes are also imposed by many subnational entities. Taxes consist of direct tax or indirect tax, and may be paid in money or as its labour equivalent (often but not always unpaid.)

a. Tax avoidance
b. Taxpayer
c. State tax levels
d. Federal Unemployment Tax Act

29. _____ is a term used in accounting, economics and finance to spread the cost of an asset over the span of several years.

In simple words we can say that _____ is the reduction in the value of an asset due to usage, passage of time, wear and tear, technological outdating or obsolescence, depletion, inadequacy, rot, rust, decay or other such factors.

In accounting, _____ is a term used to describe any method of attributing the historical or purchase cost of an asset across its useful life, roughly corresponding to normal wear and tear.

a. General ledger
b. Depreciation
c. Net profit
d. Current asset

30. A _____ is a compensation, usually financial, received by a worker in exchange for their labor.

Chapter 12. OTHER NOT-FOR-PROFIT ORGANIZATIONS

Compensation in terms of _____s is given to worker and compensation in terms of salary is given to employees. Compensation is a monetary benefits given to employees in returns of the services provided by them.

a. Wage
c. BMC Software, Inc.
b. Retirement plan
d. 3M Company

31. In the United States, _____ is health care provided for free or at reduced prices to low income patients. The percentage of doctors providing _____ dropped from 76% in 1996-97 to 68% in 2004-2005. Potential reasons for the decline include changes in physician practice patterns and increasing financial pressures.

a. BNSF Railway
c. Charity care
b. 3M Company
d. BMC Software, Inc.

32. In law, _____ is a type of negligence in which the misfeasance, malfeasance or nonfeasance of a professional, under a duty to act, fails to follow generally accepted professional standards, and that breach of duty is the proximate cause of injury to a plaintiff who suffers damages. It is committed by a professional or her/his subordinates or agents on behalf of a client or patient that causes damages to the client or patient. Perhaps the most publicized forms are medical _____ and legal _____ by medical practitioners and lawyers respectively, though _____ suits against accountants (Arthur Andersen) and investment advisors (Merrill Lynch) have featured in the news more recently.

a. Partnership
c. FCPA
b. Bylaw
d. Malpractice

33. The term _____ refers to government debt, expenditures and revenues, or to finance (particularly financial revenue) in general.

- _____ deficit is the budget deficit of federal or local government
- _____ policy is the discretionary spending of governments. Contrasts with monetary policy.
- _____ year and _____ quarter are reporting periods for firms and other agencies.

See also

- Procurator _____ and Crown Office and Procurator _____ Service

a. Scientific Research and Experimental Development Tax Incentive Program
b. Swap
c. Fiscal
d. Comparable

34. _____, in the sociological and psychological context, is the concept or idea of fairness or justice in relationships between children, youth, adults and seniors, particularly in terms of treatment and interactions. It has been studied in environmental and sociological settings. In the context of institutional investment management, _____ is the principle that an endowed institution's spending rate must not exceed its after-inflation rate of compound return, so that investment gains are spent equally on current and future constituents of the endowed assets.

a. USA Today
c. International Monetary Fund
b. Outsourcing
d. Intergenerational equity

Chapter 13. USING COST INFORMATION TO MANAGE AND CONTROL

1. Project _____: The project _____ is a prediction of the costs associated with a particular company project. These costs include labor, materials, and other related expenses. The project _____ is often broken down into specific tasks, with task _____s assigned to each.
   - a. BMC Software, Inc.
   - b. 3M Company
   - c. BNSF Railway
   - d. Budget

2. The _____ is a federal agency within the legislative branch of the United States government. It is a government agency that provides economic data to Congress. It was created by the Congressional Budget and Impoundment Control Act of 1974.
   - a. BMC Software, Inc.
   - b. Congressional Budget Office
   - c. 3M Company
   - d. General Accounting Office

3. The _____ is currently the source of generally accepted accounting principles (GAAP) used by State and Local governments in the [[United States of America]]. As with most of the entities involved in creating GAAP in the United States, it is a private, non-governmental organization.

   The _____ is subject to oversight by the Financial Accounting Foundation (FAF), which selects the members of the _____ and the Financial Accounting Standards Board, and funds both organizations.

   - a. Fannie Mae
   - b. Multinational corporation
   - c. National Conference of Commissioners on Uniform State Laws
   - d. Governmental Accounting Standards Board

4. The term _____ usually refers to a company that is permitted to offer its registered securities (stock, bonds, etc.) for sale to the general public, typically through a stock exchange, or occasionally a company whose stock is traded over the counter (OTC) via market makers who use non-exchange quotation services.

   The term '_____' may also refer to a company owned by the government.

   - a. Governmental Accounting Standards Board
   - b. Professional association
   - c. MicroStrategy
   - d. Public Company

5. The _____ (sometimes called 'Peekaboo') is a private-sector, non-profit corporation created by the Sarbanes-Oxley Act, a 2002 United States federal law, to oversee the auditors of public companies. Its stated purpose is to 'protect the interests of investors and further the public interest in the preparation of informative, fair, and independent audit reports'. Although a private entity, the _____ has many government-like regulatory functions, making it in some ways similar to the private Self Regulatory Organizations (SROs) that regulate stock markets and other aspects of the financial markets in the United States.
   - a. 3M Company
   - b. Pension Benefit Guaranty Corporation
   - c. Public Company Accounting Oversight Board
   - d. Financial Crimes Enforcement Network

6. In economics, business, retail, and accounting, a _____ is the value of money that has been used up to produce something, and hence is not available for use anymore. In economics, a _____ is an alternative that is given up as a result of a decision. In business, the _____ may be one of acquisition, in which case the amount of money expended to acquire it is counted as _____.

Chapter 13. USING COST INFORMATION TO MANAGE AND CONTROL

a. Cost of quality
b. Cost
c. Prime cost
d. Cost allocation

7. In economics and finance, _____ is the change in total cost that arises when the quantity produced changes by one unit. It is the cost of producing one more unit of a good. Mathematically, the _____ function is expressed as the first derivative of the total cost (TC) function with respect to quantity (Q.)
a. Cost of quality
b. Variable cost
c. Cost accounting
d. Marginal cost

8. _____ is concerned with the provisions and use of accounting information to managers within organizations, to provide them with the basis to make informed business decisions that will allow them to be better equipped in their management and control functions.

In contrast to financial accountancy information, _____ information is:

- usually confidential and used by management, instead of publicly reported;
- forward-looking, instead of historical;
- pragmatically computed using extensive management information systems and internal controls, instead of complying with accounting standards.

This is because of the different emphasis: _____ information is used within an organization, typically for decision-making.

a. Nonassurance services
b. Grenzplankostenrechnung
c. Management accounting
d. Governmental accounting

9. The _____ was established as the _____ by the Budget and Accounting Act of 1921 (Pub.L. 67-13, 42 Stat. 20, June 10, 1921.)
a. BMC Software, Inc.
b. 3M Company
c. GAO
d. General Accounting Office

10. A _____ is a fungible, negotiable instrument representing financial value. they are broadly categorized into debt securities (such as banknotes, bonds and debentures), and equity securities; e.g., common stocks. The company or other entity issuing the _____ is called the issuer.
a. Tracking stock
b. 3M Company
c. Security
d. BMC Software, Inc.

11. _____ in the United States currently refers to the federal Old-Age, Survivors, and Disability Insurance (OASDI) program.

Chapter 13. USING COST INFORMATION TO MANAGE AND CONTROL

The original _____ Act and the current version of the Act, as amended encompass several social welfare and social insurance programs. The larger and better known programs are:

- Federal Old-Age, Survivors, and Disability Insurance
- Unemployment benefits
- Temporary Assistance for Needy Families
- Health Insurance for Aged and Disabled (Medicare)
- Grants to States for Medical Assistance Programs (Medicaid)
- State Children's Health Insurance Program (SCHIP)
- Supplemental Security Income (Social SecurityI)

U.S. _____ is a social insurance program funded through dedicated payroll taxes called Federal Insurance Contributions Act (FICA.) Tax deposits are formally entrusted to Federal Old-Age and Survivors Insurance Trust Fund, or Federal Disability Insurance Trust Fund, Federal Hospital Insurance Trust Fund or the Federal Supplementary Medical Insurance Trust Fund.

a. Price-to-sales ratio
b. Sale
c. Comparable
d. Social Security

12. The United States _____ is an independent agency of the United States federal government that administers Social Security, a social insurance program consisting of retirement, disability, and survivors' benefits. To qualify for these benefits, most American workers pay Social Security taxes on their earnings; future benefits are based on the employees' contributions.

The _____ was established by a law currently codified at 42 U.S.C.

a. Minority interest
b. Return on assets
c. Social Security Administration
d. Time value of money

13. Under the average-cost method, it is assumed that the cost of inventory is based on the _____ of the goods available for sale during the period. _____ is computed by dividing the total cost of goods available for sale by the total units available for sale. This gives a weighted-average unit cost that is applied to the units in the ending inventory.

a. ABC Television Network
b. AIG
c. Ending inventory
d. Average cost

14. In economics, _____ are business expenses that are not dependent on the activities of the business They tend to be time-related, such as salaries or rents being paid per month. This is in contrast to variable costs, which are volume-related (and are paid per quantity.)

In management accounting, _____ are defined as expenses that do not change in proportion to the activity of a business, within the relevant period or scale of production.

Chapter 13. USING COST INFORMATION TO MANAGE AND CONTROL

a. Marginal cost
b. Cost accounting
c. Cost of quality
d. Fixed costs

15. _____s are expenses that change in proportion to the activity of a business. In other words, _____ is the sum of marginal costs. It can also be considered normal costs.

a. Fixed costs
b. Cost accounting
c. Quality costs
d. Variable cost

16. In probability theory and statistics, the _____ of a random variable, probability distribution averaging the squared distance of its possible values from the expected value (mean.) Whereas the mean is a way to describe the location of a distribution, the _____ is a way to capture its scale or degree of being spread out. The unit of _____ is the square of the unit of the original variable.

a. Monte Carlo methods
b. Time series
c. Statistics
d. Variance

17. In economics and business decision-making, _____ are costs that cannot be recovered once they have been incurred. _____ are sometimes contrasted with variable costs, which are the costs that will change due to the proposed course of action, and prospective costs which are costs that will be incurred if an action is taken.

In traditional microeconomic theory, only variable costs are relevant to a decision.

a. 3M Company
b. Sunk costs
c. BNSF Railway
d. BMC Software, Inc.

18. _____ is the term used to refer to the standard framework of guidelines for financial accounting used in any given jurisdiction. _____ includes the standards, conventions, and rules accountants follow in recording and summarizing transactions, and in the preparation of financial statements.

Financial accounting information must be assembled and reported objectively.

a. Current asset
b. Long-term liabilities
c. General ledger
d. Generally accepted accounting principles

19. In management accounting, _____ establishes budget and actual cost of operations, processes, departments or product and the analysis of variances, profitability or social use of funds. Managers use _____ to support decision-making to cut a company's costs and improve profitability. As a form of management accounting, _____ need not follow standards such as GAAP, because its primary use is for internal managers, rather than outside users, and what to compute is instead decided pragmatically.

a. Prime cost
b. Cost-volume-profit analysis
c. Cost accounting
d. Marginal cost

20. The _____ is a Cabinet-level office, and is the largest office within the Executive Office of the President of the United States (EOP.) It is an important conduit by which the White House oversees the activities of federal agencies. OMB is tasked with giving expert advice to senior White House officials on a range of topics relating to federal policy, management, legislative, regulatory, and budgetary issues.

Chapter 13. USING COST INFORMATION TO MANAGE AND CONTROL

a. Office of Management and Budget
c. Alaska Air Group
b. Analysis of variance
d. AT'T Wireless Services, Inc.

21. _____ is subcontracting a process, such as product design or manufacturing, to a third-party company. The decision to outsource is often made in the interest of lowering cost or making better use of time and energy costs, redirecting or conserving energy directed at the competencies of a particular business, or to make more efficient use of land, labor, capital, (information) technology and resources. _____ became part of the business lexicon during the 1980s.
a. Outsourcing
c. USA Today
b. US Airways, Inc.
d. Economic Growth and Tax Relief Reconciliation Act of 2001

22. _____ is the incidence or process of transferring ownership of a business, enterprise, agency or public service from the public sector (government) to the private sector (business.) In a broader sense, privatisation refers to transfer of any government function to the private sector including governmental functions like revenue collection and law enforcement.

The term 'Privatisation' also has been used to describe two unrelated transactions.

a. BMC Software, Inc.
c. BNSF Railway
b. Privatization
d. 3M Company

23. The _____ after Senator Harold Burton of Ohio and Senator Lister Hill of Alabama, is a United States federal law passed in 1946. This act responded to the first of Trumane;s proposals and was designed to provide federal grants and guaranteed loans to improve the physical plant of the natione;s hospital system. Money was designated to the states to achieve 4.5 beds per 1,000 people.
a. Lease
c. Model Code of Professional Responsibility
b. Tax patent
d. Hospital Survey and Construction Act

24. _____ is one of the four Ps of the marketing mix. The other three aspects are product, promotion, and place. It is also a key variable in microeconomic price allocation theory.
a. Pricing
c. Target costing
b. Cost-plus pricing
d. Price

25. _____ accounting (Full costA) generally refers to the process of collecting and presenting information (costs as well as advantages) for each proposed alternative when a decision is necessary. A synonym, true cost accounting (TCA) is also often used. Experts consider both terms problematic as definitions of 'true' and 'full' are inherently subjective
a. BMC Software, Inc.
c. 3M Company
b. Full cost
d. BNSF Railway

26. _____ is a costing model that identifies activities in an organization and assigns the cost of each activity resource to all products and services according to the actual consumption by each: it assigns more indirect costs (overhead) into direct costs.

In this way an organization can establish the true cost of its individual products and services for the purposes of identifying and eliminating those which are unprofitable and lowering the prices of those which are overpriced.

Chapter 13. USING COST INFORMATION TO MANAGE AND CONTROL

In a business organization, the ABC methodology assigns an organization's resource costs through activities to the products and services provided to its customers.

a. Indirect costs
b. ABC Television Network
c. Activity-based management
d. Activity-based costing

27. _____ are costs that are not directly accountable to a particular function or product. _____ may be either fixed or variable. _____ include taxes, administration, personnel and security costs, and are also known as overhead.

a. ABC Television Network
b. Activity-based costing
c. Activity-based management
d. Indirect costs

28. In business, _____, Overhead cost or _____ expense refers to an ongoing expense of operating a business. The term _____ is usually used to group expenses that are necessary to the continued functioning of the business, but do not directly generate profits.

_____ expenses are all costs on the income statement except for direct labor and direct materials.

a. Overhead
b. ABC Television Network
c. Intangible assets
d. AIG

29. The _____ is the national, professional association of CPAs in the United States, with more than 330,000 members, including CPAs in business and industry, public practice, government, and education; student affiliates; and international associates. It sets ethical standards for the profession and U.S. auditing standards for audits of private companies; federal, state and local governments; and non-profit organizations.

Approximately 40% of its members are engaged in the practice of public accounting, in areas such as auditing, accounting, taxation, general business consulting, business valuation, personal financial planning and business technology.

a. AIG
b. Other postemployment benefits
c. American Institute of Certified Public Accountants
d. ABC Television Network

30. _____ are formal records of a business' financial activities.

In British English, including United Kingdom company law, _____ are often referred to as accounts, although the term _____ is also used, particularly by accountants.

_____ provide an overview of a business' financial condition in both short and long term.

a. Notes to the financial statements
b. Statement of retained earnings
c. Financial statements
d. 3M Company

31. _____ is an accounting system often used by nonprofit organizations and by the public sector. According to StartHereGoPlaces, _____ is a '[m]ethod of accounting and presentation whereby assets and liabilities are grouped according to the purpose for which they are to be used.'

_____ serves any nonprofit organization or the public sector. These organizations have a need for special reporting to financial statements users that show how money is spent, rather than how much profit was earned.

a. Refunding
c. Replacement cost
b. Liquidating dividend
d. Fund accounting

Chapter 14. MANAGING FOR RESULTS

1. The _____ is currently the source of generally accepted accounting principles (GAAP) used by State and Local governments in the [[United States of America]]. As with most of the entities involved in creating GAAP in the United States, it is a private, non-governmental organization.

The _____ is subject to oversight by the Financial Accounting Foundation (FAF), which selects the members of the _____ and the Financial Accounting Standards Board, and funds both organizations.

   a. Fannie Mae
   b. Multinational corporation
   c. National Conference of Commissioners on Uniform State Laws
   d. Governmental Accounting Standards Board

2. The _____ was established as the _____ by the Budget and Accounting Act of 1921 (Pub.L. 67-13, 42 Stat. 20, June 10, 1921.)
   a. 3M Company
   b. GAO
   c. General Accounting Office
   d. BMC Software, Inc.

3. The term _____ usually refers to a company that is permitted to offer its registered securities (stock, bonds, etc.) for sale to the general public, typically through a stock exchange, or occasionally a company whose stock is traded over the counter (OTC) via market makers who use non-exchange quotation services.

The term '_____' may also refer to a company owned by the government.

   a. MicroStrategy
   b. Governmental Accounting Standards Board
   c. Public Company
   d. Professional association

4. The _____ (sometimes called 'Peekaboo') is a private-sector, non-profit corporation created by the Sarbanes-Oxley Act, a 2002 United States federal law, to oversee the auditors of public companies. Its stated purpose is to 'protect the interests of investors and further the public interest in the preparation of informative, fair, and independent audit reports'. Although a private entity, the _____ has many government-like regulatory functions, making it in some ways similar to the private Self Regulatory Organizations (SROs) that regulate stock markets and other aspects of the financial markets in the United States.
   a. Pension Benefit Guaranty Corporation
   b. 3M Company
   c. Financial Crimes Enforcement Network
   d. Public Company Accounting Oversight Board

5. An _____ is a practitioner of accountancy, which is the measurement, disclosure or provision of assurance about financial information that helps managers, investors, tax authorities and other decision makers make resource allocation decisions.

The word '_____' is derived from the French 'Compter' which took its origin from the Latin 'Computare'. The word was formerly written in English as 'Accomptant', but in process of time the word, which was always pronounced by dropping the 'p', became gradually changed both in pronunciation and in orthography to its present form.

   a. ABC Television Network
   b. AIG
   c. AMEX
   d. Accountant

Chapter 14. MANAGING FOR RESULTS

6. _____ is a term that refers both to:

- a formal discipline used to help appraise, or assess, the case for a project or proposal, which itself is a process known as project appraisal; and
- an informal approach to making decisions of any kind.

Under both definitions the process involves, whether explicitly or implicitly, weighing the total expected costs against the total expected benefits of one or more actions in order to choose the best or most profitable option. The formal process is often referred to as either CBA (_____) or BCost-benefit analysis

A hallmark of CBA is that all benefits and all costs are expressed in money terms, and are adjusted for the time value of money, so that all flows of benefits and flows of project costs over time (which tend to occur at different points in time) are expressed on a common basis in terms of their 'e;present value.'e; Closely related, but slightly different, formal techniques include Cost-effectiveness analysis, Economic impact analysis, Fiscal impact analysis and Social Return on Investment(SROI) analysis. The latter builds upon the logic of _____, but differs in that it is explicitly designed to inform the practical decision-making of enterprise managers and investors focused on optimising their social and environmental impacts.

a. BMC Software, Inc.
b. BNSF Railway
c. 3M Company
d. Cost-benefit analysis

7. Project _____: The project _____ is a prediction of the costs associated with a particular company project. These costs include labor, materials, and other related expenses. The project _____ is often broken down into specific tasks, with task _____s assigned to each.

a. BMC Software, Inc.
b. 3M Company
c. BNSF Railway
d. Budget

8. _____ is that which is owed; usually referencing assets owed, but the term can also cover moral obligations and other interactions not requiring money. In the case of assets, _____ is a means of using future purchasing power in the present before a summation has been earned. Some companies and corporations use _____ as a part of their overall corporate finance strategy.

a. Debt
b. Lender
c. Loan
d. Debenture

9. In economic models, the _____ time frame assumes no fixed factors of production. Firms can enter or leave the marketplace, and the cost (and availability) of land, labor, raw materials, and capital goods can be assumed to vary. In contrast, in the short-run time frame, certain factors are assumed to be fixed, because there is not sufficient time for them to change.

a. Short-run
b. BMC Software, Inc.
c. 3M Company
d. Long-run

10. _____ is concerned with the provisions and use of accounting information to managers within organizations, to provide them with the basis to make informed business decisions that will allow them to be better equipped in their management and control functions.

Chapter 14. MANAGING FOR RESULTS

In contrast to financial accountancy information, _____ information is:

- usually confidential and used by management, instead of publicly reported;
- forward-looking, instead of historical;
- pragmatically computed using extensive management information systems and internal controls, instead of complying with accounting standards.

This is because of the different emphasis: _____ information is used within an organization, typically for decision-making.

a. Nonassurance services
b. Governmental accounting
c. Grenzplankostenrechnung
d. Management accounting

11. _____ is a demonstration of a process -- such as a variable, term, or object -- relative in terms of the specific process or set of validation tests used to determine its presence and quantity. Properties described in this manner must be sufficiently accessible, so that persons other than the definer may independently measure or test for them at will. An _____ is generally designed to model a conceptual definition.

a. AMEX
b. ABC Television Network
c. Operational definition
d. AIG

12. The _____ is a federal agency within the legislative branch of the United States government. It is a government agency that provides economic data to Congress. It was created by the Congressional Budget and Impoundment Control Act of 1974.

a. BMC Software, Inc.
b. General Accounting Office
c. 3M Company
d. Congressional Budget Office

13. A _____ is a compensation, usually financial, received by a worker in exchange for their labor.

Compensation in terms of _____s is given to worker and compensation in terms of salary is given to employees. Compensation is a monetary benefits given to employees in returns of the services provided by them.

a. Retirement plan
b. Wage
c. BMC Software, Inc.
d. 3M Company

14. _____ is a technique of planning and decision-making which reverses the working process of traditional budgeting. In traditional incremental budgeting, departmental managers justify only increases over the previous year budget and what has been already spent is automatically sanctioned. No reference is made to the previous level of expenditure.

a. BMC Software, Inc.
b. BNSF Railway
c. 3M Company
d. Zero-based budgeting

15. The _____ after Senator Harold Burton of Ohio and Senator Lister Hill of Alabama, is a United States federal law passed in 1946. This act responded to the first of Trumane;s proposals and was designed to provide federal grants and guaranteed loans to improve the physical plant of the natione;s hospital system. Money was designated to the states to achieve 4.5 beds per 1,000 people.

Chapter 14. MANAGING FOR RESULTS

a. Lease
b. Model Code of Professional Responsibility
c. Tax patent
d. Hospital Survey and Construction Act

16. _____ is the process whereby an organization establishes the parameters within which programs, investments, and acquisitions are reaching the desired results. Performance Reference Model of the Federal Enterprise Architecture, 2005.

This process of measuring performance often requires the use of statistical evidence to determine progress toward specific defined organizational objectives.

There are many types of measurements.

a. Performance measurement
b. Management by objectives
c. Trustee
d. Management by exception

17. The _____ is the national, professional association of CPAs in the United States, with more than 330,000 members, including CPAs in business and industry, public practice, government, and education; student affiliates; and international associates. It sets ethical standards for the profession and U.S. auditing standards for audits of private companies; federal, state and local governments; and non-profit organizations.

Approximately 40% of its members are engaged in the practice of public accounting, in areas such as auditing, accounting, taxation, general business consulting, business valuation, personal financial planning and business technology.

a. Other postemployment benefits
b. American Institute of Certified Public Accountants
c. AIG
d. ABC Television Network

18. The _____ is a United States law enacted in 1993. It is one of a series of laws designed to improve government project management. The GPRA requires agencies to engage in project management tasks such as setting goals, measuring results, and reporting their progress.

a. 3M Company
b. BMC Software, Inc.
c. BNSF Railway
d. Government Performance and Results Act

19. In business and accounting, _____ are everything of value that is owned by a person or company. It is a claim on the property your income of a borrower. The balance sheet of a firm records the monetary value of the _____ owned by the firm.

a. Accrual basis accounting
b. Accounts receivable
c. Earnings before interest, taxes, depreciation and amortization
d. Assets

20. In economics, _____ or _____ goods or real _____ refers to factors of production used to create goods or services that are not themselves significantly consumed (though they may depreciate) in the production process. _____ goods may be acquired with money or financial _____. In finance and accounting, _____ generally refers to financial wealth, especially that used to start or maintain a business.

Chapter 14. MANAGING FOR RESULTS

a. Vyborg Appeal
c. Screening

b. Disclosure
d. Capital

21. The term _____ has three unrelated technical definitions, and is also used in a variety of non-technical ways.

- In financial economics, it refers to any asset used to make money, as opposed to assets used for personal enjoyment or consumption. This is an important distinction because two people can disagree sharply about the value of personal assets, one person might think a sports car is more valuable than a pickup truck, another person might have the opposite taste. But if an asset is held for the purpose of making money, taste has nothing to do with it, only differences of opinion about how much money the asset will produce. With the further assumption that people agree on the probability distribution of future cash flows, it is possible to have an objective _____ pricing model. Even without the assumption of agreement, it is possible to set rational limits on _____ value.
- In governmental accounting, it is defined as any asset used in operations with an initial useful life extending beyond one reporting period. Generally, government managers have a 'stewardship' duty to maintain _____s under their control. See International Public Sector Accounting Standards for details.
- In US tax accounting, it is defined as any property other than a list of exceptions. The main exceptions are anything held for sale, and any real estate or depreciable property used in business. Almost everything you own and use for personal purposes, pleasure or investment is a _____. If something is a _____ for tax purposes, gains or losses on sale or disposition are capital gains or capital losses. For individuals, however, capital losses on property held for personal use are generally not deductible. See the IRS publication Tax Facts about Capital Gains and Losses for details.

A well-known financial accounting textbook advises that the term be avoided except in tax accounting because it is used in so many different senses, not all of them well-defined. For example it is often used as a synonym for fixed assets or for investments in securities.

A common non-technical usage occurs when people ask that employees or the environment or something else be treated as a _____.

a. BMC Software, Inc.
c. Solvency

b. 3M Company
d. Capital asset

Chapter 15. AUDITING GOVERNMENTS AND NOT-FOR-PROFIT ORGANIZATIONS

1. The general definition of an _____ is an evaluation of a person, organization, system, process, project or product. _____s are performed to ascertain the validity and reliability of information; also to provide an assessment of a system's internal control. The goal of an _____ is to express an opinion on the person/organization/system (etc) in question, under evaluation based on work done on a test basis.
   a. Audit regime
   b. Institute of Chartered Accountants of India
   c. Assurance service
   d. Audit

2. The _____ of a company or public agency is the corporate officer primarily responsible for managing the financial risks of the business or agency. This officer is also responsible for financial planning and record-keeping, as well as financial reporting to higher management. (In recent years, however, the role has expanded to encompass communicating financial performance and forecasts to the analyst community.)
   a. Chief executive officer
   b. NASDAQ
   c. Chief Financial Officer
   d. Merck ' Co., Inc.

3. The _____ signed into law by President George H.W. Bush on November 15, 1990, is a United States federal law intended to improve the government's financial management, outlining standards of financial performance and disclosure. Among other measures, the Office of Management and Budget (OMB) was given greater authority over federal financial management. For each of 23 federal departments and agencies, the position of chief financial officer was created.
   a. Bylaw
   b. Scottish Poor Laws
   c. Jenkins Committee
   d. Chief Financial Officers Act of 1990

4. The _____ is currently the source of generally accepted accounting principles (GAAP) used by State and Local governments in the [[United States of America]]. As with most of the entities involved in creating GAAP in the United States, it is a private, non-governmental organization.

   The _____ is subject to oversight by the Financial Accounting Foundation (FAF), which selects the members of the _____ and the Financial Accounting Standards Board, and funds both organizations.

   a. National Conference of Commissioners on Uniform State Laws
   b. Multinational corporation
   c. Fannie Mae
   d. Governmental Accounting Standards Board

5. In economics, the concept of the _____ refers to the decision-making time frame of a firm in which at least one factor of production is fixed. Costs which are fixed in the _____ have no impact on a firms decisions. For example a firm can raise output by increasing the amount of labour through overtime.
   a. BMC Software, Inc.
   b. Long-run
   c. Short-run
   d. 3M Company

6. The _____ is the national, professional association of CPAs in the United States, with more than 330,000 members, including CPAs in business and industry, public practice, government, and education; student affiliates; and international associates. It sets ethical standards for the profession and U.S. auditing standards for audits of private companies; federal, state and local governments; and non-profit organizations.

Approximately 40% of its members are engaged in the practice of public accounting, in areas such as auditing, accounting, taxation, general business consulting, business valuation, personal financial planning and business technology.

Chapter 15. AUDITING GOVERNMENTS AND NOT-FOR-PROFIT ORGANIZATIONS

a. Other postemployment benefits
b. AIG
c. American Institute of Certified Public Accountants
d. ABC Television Network

7. An _____ is a comprehensive report on a company's activities throughout the preceding year. _____s are intended to give shareholders and other interested persons information about the company's activities and financial performance. Most jurisdictions require companies to prepare and disclose _____s, and many require the _____ to be filed at the company's registry.
   a. AMEX
   b. ABC Television Network
   c. AIG
   d. Annual Report

8. Project _____: The project _____ is a prediction of the costs associated with a particular company project. These costs include labor, materials, and other related expenses. The project _____ is often broken down into specific tasks, with task _____s assigned to each.
   a. BMC Software, Inc.
   b. Budget
   c. 3M Company
   d. BNSF Railway

9. The _____ is the director of the Government Accountability Office (GAO, formerly known as the General Accounting Office), a legislative branch agency founded by Congress in 1921 to ensure the fiscal and managerial accountability of the federal government.

The Comptroller General is appointed for a fifteen-year term by the President of the United States with the advice and consent of the Senate per 31 U.S.C. § 703.

   a. BMC Software, Inc.
   b. 3M Company
   c. Comptroller General of the United States
   d. BNSF Railway

10. The _____ is a private, not-for-profit organization whose primary purpose is to develop generally accepted accounting principles (GAAP) within the United States in the public's interest. The Securities and Exchange Commission (SEC) designated the _____ as the organization responsible for setting accounting standards for public companies in the U.S. It was created in 1973, replacing the Accounting Principles Board and the Committee on Accounting Procedure of the American Institute of Certified Public Accountants. The _____'s mission is 'to establish and improve standards of financial accounting and reporting for the guidance and education of the public, including issuers, auditors, and users of financial information.'

The _____ is not a governmental body.

   a. Governmental Accounting Standards Board
   b. Financial Accounting Standards Board
   c. Fannie Mae
   d. Public company

11. The _____ was established as the _____ by the Budget and Accounting Act of 1921 (Pub.L. 67-13, 42 Stat. 20, June 10, 1921.)
   a. GAO
   b. 3M Company
   c. BMC Software, Inc.
   d. General Accounting Office

Chapter 15. AUDITING GOVERNMENTS AND NOT-FOR-PROFIT ORGANIZATIONS

12. The _____ is a Cabinet-level office, and is the largest office within the Executive Office of the President of the United States (EOP.) It is an important conduit by which the White House oversees the activities of federal agencies. OMB is tasked with giving expert advice to senior White House officials on a range of topics relating to federal policy, management, legislative, regulatory, and budgetary issues.
    a. Office of Management and Budget
    b. AT'T Wireless Services, Inc.
    c. Alaska Air Group
    d. Analysis of variance

13. The _____ of 2002 (Pub.L. 107-204, 116 Stat. 745, enacted July 30, 2002), also known as the Public Company Accounting Reform and Investor Protection Act of 2002, is a United States federal law enacted on July 30, 2002 in response to a number of major corporate and accounting scandals including those affecting Enron, Tyco International, Adelphia, Peregrine Systems and WorldCom. The legislation establishes new or enhanced standards for all U.S. public company boards, management, and public accounting firms. It does not apply to privately held companies.
    a. FCPA
    b. Lease
    c. Fair Labor Standards Act
    d. Sarbanes-Oxley Act

14. A _____ an audit of financial statements, is the review of the financial statements of a company or any other legal entity (including governments), resulting in the publication of an independent opinion on whether or not those financial statements are relevant, accurate, complete, and fairly presented. _____s are typically performed by firms of practicing accountants due to the specialist financial reporting knowledge they require. The _____ is one of many assurance or attestation functions provided by accounting and auditing firms, whereby the firm provides an independent opinion on published information.
    a. Management representation
    b. Mainframe audit
    c. Lead Auditor
    d. Financial audit

15. _____ is a demonstration of a process -- such as a variable, term, or object -- relative in terms of the specific process or set of validation tests used to determine its presence and quantity. Properties described in this manner must be sufficiently accessible, so that persons other than the definer may independently measure or test for them at will. An _____ is generally designed to model a conceptual definition.
    a. Operational definition
    b. ABC Television Network
    c. AIG
    d. AMEX

16. _____ refers to an examination of a program, function, operation or the management systems and procedures of a governmental or non-profit entity to assess whether the entity is achieving economy, efficiency and effectiveness in the employment of available resources. The examination is objective and systematic, generally using structured and professionally adopted methodologies.

In most countries, _____s of governmental activities are carried out by the external audit bodies at federal or state level.

    a. Statements on Auditing Standards
    b. Trustworthy Repositories Audit ' Certification
    c. Mainframe audit
    d. Performance audit

17. _____ is the term used to refer to the standard framework of guidelines for financial accounting used in any given jurisdiction. _____ includes the standards, conventions, and rules accountants follow in recording and summarizing transactions, and in the preparation of financial statements.

Financial accounting information must be assembled and reported objectively.

a. Generally accepted accounting principles
b. Current asset
c. General ledger
d. Long-term liabilities

18. _____ are ten auditing standards, developed by the AICPA, consisting of general standards, standards of field work, and standards of reporting, along with interpretations. They were developed by the AICPA in 1947 and have undergone minor changes since then.

The _____ are as follows:

1. The auditor must have adequate technical training and proficiency to perform the audit
2. The auditor must maintain independence in mental attitude in all matters related to the audit.
3. The auditor must use due professional care during the performance of the audit and the preparation of the report.

1. The auditor must adequately plan the work and must properly supervise any assistants.
2. The auditor must obtain a sufficient understanding of the entity and its environment, including its internal control, to assess the risk of material misstatement of the financial statements whether due to error or fraud, and to design the nature, timing, and extent of further audit procedures.
3. The auditor must obtain sufficient appropriate audit evidence by performing audit procedures to afford a reasonable basis for an opinion regarding the financial statements under audit.

The new standards are in effect for audits of financial statements for periods beginning on or after December 15, 2006.

1. The auditor must state in the auditor's report whether the financial statements are in accordance with generally accepted accounting principles (GAAP.)
2. The auditor must identify in the auditor's report those circumstances in which such principles have not been consistently observed in the current period in relation to the preceding period.
3. When the auditor determines that informative disclosures are not reasonably adequate, the auditor must so state in the auditor's report.
4. The auditor must either express an opinion regarding the financial statements, taken as a whole the auditor should state the reasons therefore in the auditor's report. In all cases where the auditor's name is associated with the financial statements, the auditor should clearly indicate the character of the auditor's work, if any, and the degree of responsibility the auditor is taking, in the auditor's report.

a. Joint audit
b. Continuous auditing
c. Negative assurance
d. Generally accepted auditing standards

Chapter 15. AUDITING GOVERNMENTS AND NOT-FOR-PROFIT ORGANIZATIONS

19. The _____ after Senator Harold Burton of Ohio and Senator Lister Hill of Alabama, is a United States federal law passed in 1946. This act responded to the first of Trumane;s proposals and was designed to provide federal grants and guaranteed loans to improve the physical plant of the natione;s hospital system. Money was designated to the states to achieve 4.5 beds per 1,000 people.

a. Tax patent
b. Lease
c. Model Code of Professional Responsibility
d. Hospital Survey and Construction Act

20. In the United States, _____ federal benefits is defined as any federal program, project, service, and activity provided by the federal government that directly assists or benefits the American public in the areas of education, health, public safety, public welfare, and public works, among others. The assistance, which can reach to over $400 billion dollars annually, is provided and administered by federal government agencies, such as the U.S. Department of Housing and Urban Development and the U.S. Department of Health and Human Services, through special programs to recipients.

The term assistance is defined by the federal government as:

In order to provide _____ in an organized manner, the federal government provides assistance through federal agencies.

a. 3M Company
b. BMC Software, Inc.
c. BNSF Railway
d. Federal assistance

21. The _____ is a federal agency within the legislative branch of the United States government. It is a government agency that provides economic data to Congress. It was created by the Congressional Budget and Impoundment Control Act of 1974.

a. General Accounting Office
b. 3M Company
c. BMC Software, Inc.
d. Congressional Budget Office

Chapter 16. FEDERAL GOVERNMENT ACCOUNTING

1. The _____ of a company or public agency is the corporate officer primarily responsible for managing the financial risks of the business or agency. This officer is also responsible for financial planning and record-keeping, as well as financial reporting to higher management. (In recent years, however, the role has expanded to encompass communicating financial performance and forecasts to the analyst community.)
    a. Merck ' Co., Inc.
    b. NASDAQ
    c. Chief executive officer
    d. Chief Financial Officer

2. The _____ signed into law by President George H.W. Bush on November 15, 1990, is a United States federal law intended to improve the government's financial management, outlining standards of financial performance and disclosure. Among other measures, the Office of Management and Budget (OMB) was given greater authority over federal financial management. For each of 23 federal departments and agencies, the position of chief financial officer was created.
    a. Bylaw
    b. Scottish Poor Laws
    c. Jenkins Committee
    d. Chief Financial Officers Act of 1990

3. The _____ is an executive department and the treasury of the United States federal government. It was established by an Act of Congress in 1789 to manage government revenue. The Department is administered by the Secretary of the Treasury, who is a member of the Cabinet.
    a. Sale
    b. Department of the Treasury
    c. Help desk and incident reporting auditing
    d. Serial bonds

4. The _____ is a private, not-for-profit organization whose primary purpose is to develop generally accepted accounting principles (GAAP) within the United States in the public's interest. The Securities and Exchange Commission (SEC) designated the _____ as the organization responsible for setting accounting standards for public companies in the U.S. It was created in 1973, replacing the Accounting Principles Board and the Committee on Accounting Procedure of the American Institute of Certified Public Accountants. The _____'s mission is 'to establish and improve standards of financial accounting and reporting for the guidance and education of the public, including issuers, auditors, and users of financial information.'

The _____ is not a governmental body.

    a. Public company
    b. Fannie Mae
    c. Financial Accounting Standards Board
    d. Governmental Accounting Standards Board

5. The _____ is currently the source of generally accepted accounting principles (GAAP) used by State and Local governments in the [[United States of America]]. As with most of the entities involved in creating GAAP in the United States, it is a private, non-governmental organization.

The _____ is subject to oversight by the Financial Accounting Foundation (FAF), which selects the members of the _____ and the Financial Accounting Standards Board, and funds both organizations.

    a. Fannie Mae
    b. Multinational corporation
    c. National Conference of Commissioners on Uniform State Laws
    d. Governmental Accounting Standards Board

6. The _____ is a United States law enacted in 1993. It is one of a series of laws designed to improve government project management. The GPRA requires agencies to engage in project management tasks such as setting goals, measuring results, and reporting their progress.

Chapter 16. FEDERAL GOVERNMENT ACCOUNTING

a. 3M Company
c. BNSF Railway
b. BMC Software, Inc.
d. Government Performance and Results Act

7. The _____ after Senator Harold Burton of Ohio and Senator Lister Hill of Alabama, is a United States federal law passed in 1946. This act responded to the first of Trumane;s proposals and was designed to provide federal grants and guaranteed loans to improve the physical plant of the natione;s hospital system. Money was designated to the states to achieve 4.5 beds per 1,000 people.

a. Lease
c. Tax patent
b. Hospital Survey and Construction Act
d. Model Code of Professional Responsibility

8. The _____ duty is a legal relationship of confidence or trust between two or more parties, most commonly a _____ or trustee and a principal or beneficiary. One party, for example a corporate trust company or the trust department of a bank, holds a _____ relation or acts in a _____ capacity to another, such as one whose funds are entrusted to it for investment. In a _____ relation one person justifiably reposes confidence, good faith, reliance and trust in another whose aid, advice or protection is sought in some matter.

a. Robinson-Patman Act
c. Staple right
b. FCPA
d. Fiduciary

9. _____ are formal records of a business' financial activities.

In British English, including United Kingdom company law, _____ are often referred to as accounts, although the term _____ is also used, particularly by accountants.

_____ provide an overview of a business' financial condition in both short and long term.

a. 3M Company
c. Notes to the financial statements
b. Financial statements
d. Statement of retained earnings

10. _____ are annual financial statements or reports for the year. The financial statements, in contrast to budget, present the revenue collected and amounts spent. The _____ usually include a statement of activities (similar to an income statement in the private sector), a balance sheet and often some type of reconciliation.

a. BMC Software, Inc.
c. 3M Company
b. BNSF Railway
d. Government financial statements

11. _____, in the sociological and psychological context, is the concept or idea of fairness or justice in relationships between children, youth, adults and seniors, particularly in terms of treatment and interactions. It has been studied in environmental and sociological settings. In the context of institutional investment management, _____ is the principle that an endowed institution's spending rate must not exceed its after-inflation rate of compound return, so that investment gains are spent equally on current and future constituents of the endowed assets.

a. International Monetary Fund
c. Outsourcing
b. USA Today
d. Intergenerational equity

12. To tax is to impose a financial charge or other levy upon a _____ by a state or the functional equivalent of a state.

Taxes are also imposed by many subnational entities. Taxes consist of direct tax or indirect tax, and may be paid in money or as its labour equivalent (often but not always unpaid).

Chapter 16. FEDERAL GOVERNMENT ACCOUNTING

a. Federal Unemployment Tax Act
b. Taxpayer
c. Tax avoidance
d. State tax levels

13. Project _____: The project _____ is a prediction of the costs associated with a particular company project. These costs include labor, materials, and other related expenses. The project _____ is often broken down into specific tasks, with task _____s assigned to each.
   a. 3M Company
   b. Budget
   c. BNSF Railway
   d. BMC Software, Inc.

14. The _____ is a Cabinet-level office, and is the largest office within the Executive Office of the President of the United States (EOP.) It is an important conduit by which the White House oversees the activities of federal agencies. OMB is tasked with giving expert advice to senior White House officials on a range of topics relating to federal policy, management, legislative, regulatory, and budgetary issues.
   a. Analysis of variance
   b. Alaska Air Group
   c. AT'T Wireless Services, Inc.
   d. Office of Management and Budget

15. _____ is the act of taking possession of or assigning purpose to properties or ideas and is important in many topics, including:

   - _____ in relation to the spread of knowledge
   - _____ (art)
     - _____ (music) in reference to the re-use and proliferation of different types of music
   - _____ (economics) origination of human ownership of previously unowned natural resources such as land
   - _____ (law) as a component of government spending
   - Cultural _____ is the borrowing, or theft, of an element of cultural expression of one group by another.
   - The tort of _____ is one form of invasion of privacy.

   a. Annuity
   b. Improvement
   c. Appropriation
   d. Intangible

16. The _____ was established as the _____ by the Budget and Accounting Act of 1921 (Pub.L. 67-13, 42 Stat. 20, June 10, 1921.)
   a. 3M Company
   b. GAO
   c. BMC Software, Inc.
   d. General Accounting Office

17. The term _____ usually refers to a company that is permitted to offer its registered securities (stock, bonds, etc.) for sale to the general public, typically through a stock exchange, or occasionally a company whose stock is traded over the counter (OTC) via market makers who use non-exchange quotation services.

The term '_____' may also refer to a company owned by the government.

   a. Governmental Accounting Standards Board
   b. Public Company
   c. MicroStrategy
   d. Professional association

Chapter 16. FEDERAL GOVERNMENT ACCOUNTING

18. The _____ (sometimes called 'Peekaboo') is a private-sector, non-profit corporation created by the Sarbanes-Oxley Act, a 2002 United States federal law, to oversee the auditors of public companies. Its stated purpose is to 'protect the interests of investors and further the public interest in the preparation of informative, fair, and independent audit reports'. Although a private entity, the _____ has many government-like regulatory functions, making it in some ways similar to the private Self Regulatory Organizations (SROs) that regulate stock markets and other aspects of the financial markets in the United States.
 a. 3M Company
 b. Financial Crimes Enforcement Network
 c. Public Company Accounting Oversight Board
 d. Pension Benefit Guaranty Corporation

19. The _____ is the national, professional association of CPAs in the United States, with more than 330,000 members, including CPAs in business and industry, public practice, government, and education; student affiliates; and international associates. It sets ethical standards for the profession and U.S. auditing standards for audits of private companies; federal, state and local governments; and non-profit organizations.

Approximately 40% of its members are engaged in the practice of public accounting, in areas such as auditing, accounting, taxation, general business consulting, business valuation, personal financial planning and business technology.

 a. ABC Television Network
 b. AIG
 c. Other postemployment benefits
 d. American Institute of Certified Public Accountants

20. The _____ is a federal agency within the legislative branch of the United States government. It is a government agency that provides economic data to Congress. It was created by the Congressional Budget and Impoundment Control Act of 1974.
 a. General Accounting Office
 b. BMC Software, Inc.
 c. Congressional Budget Office
 d. 3M Company

21. A _____ is a fungible, negotiable instrument representing financial value. they are broadly categorized into debt securities (such as banknotes, bonds and debentures), and equity securities; e.g., common stocks. The company or other entity issuing the _____ is called the issuer.
 a. Tracking stock
 b. BMC Software, Inc.
 c. 3M Company
 d. Security

22. _____ in the United States currently refers to the federal Old-Age, Survivors, and Disability Insurance (OASDI) program.

Chapter 16. FEDERAL GOVERNMENT ACCOUNTING

The original _____ Act and the current version of the Act, as amended encompass several social welfare and social insurance programs. The larger and better known programs are:

- Federal Old-Age, Survivors, and Disability Insurance
- Unemployment benefits
- Temporary Assistance for Needy Families
- Health Insurance for Aged and Disabled (Medicare)
- Grants to States for Medical Assistance Programs (Medicaid)
- State Children's Health Insurance Program (SCHIP)
- Supplemental Security Income (Social Securityl)

U.S. _____ is a social insurance program funded through dedicated payroll taxes called Federal Insurance Contributions Act (FICA.) Tax deposits are formally entrusted to Federal Old-Age and Survivors Insurance Trust Fund, or Federal Disability Insurance Trust Fund, Federal Hospital Insurance Trust Fund or the Federal Supplementary Medical Insurance Trust Fund.

a. Sale
b. Comparable
c. Price-to-sales ratio
d. Social Security

23. The United States _____ is an independent agency of the United States federal government that administers Social Security, a social insurance program consisting of retirement, disability, and survivors' benefits. To qualify for these benefits, most American workers pay Social Security taxes on their earnings; future benefits are based on the employees' contributions.

The _____ was established by a law currently codified at 42 U.S.C.

a. Minority interest
b. Social Security Administration
c. Return on assets
d. Time value of money

24. _____ is the term used in the United States to designate a unique charge government units can assess against real estate parcels for certain public projects. This charge is levied in a specific geographic area known as a _____ District (S.A.D.). A _____ may only be levied against parcels of real estate which have been identified as having received a direct and unique 'benefit' from the public project.Kadzban v City of Grandville, 502 N.W.2d 299, 501; Davies v City of Lawrence, 218 Kan.

a. Malcolm Baldrige National Quality Award
b. Tax Analysts
c. Fixed tax
d. Special assessment

25. An _____ is a comprehensive report on a company's activities throughout the preceding year. _____s are intended to give shareholders and other interested persons information about the company's activities and financial performance. Most jurisdictions require companies to prepare and disclose _____s, and many require the _____ to be filed at the company's registry.

a. ABC Television Network
b. AIG
c. AMEX
d. Annual Report

Chapter 16. FEDERAL GOVERNMENT ACCOUNTING

26. The word _____ indicates that a party, or proprietor, exercises private ownership, control or use over an item of property
    a. BMC Software, Inc.
    b. BNSF Railway
    c. Proprietary
    d. 3M Company

27. An _____ is a tax levied on the financial income of people, corporations, or other legal entities. Various _____ systems exist, with varying degrees of tax incidence. Income taxation can be progressive, proportional, or regressive.
    a. Implied level of government service
    b. Income tax
    c. Individual Retirement Arrangement
    d. Ordinary income

28. In economics, _____ or _____ goods or real _____ refers to factors of production used to create goods or services that are not themselves significantly consumed (though they may depreciate) in the production process. _____ goods may be acquired with money or financial _____. In finance and accounting, _____ generally refers to financial wealth, especially that used to start or maintain a business.
    a. Vyborg Appeal
    b. Capital
    c. Screening
    d. Disclosure

29. An _____ is a practitioner of accountancy, which is the measurement, disclosure or provision of assurance about financial information that helps managers, investors, tax authorities and other decision makers make resource allocation decisions.

The word '_____' is derived from the French 'Compter' which took its origin from the Latin 'Computare'. The word was formerly written in English as 'Accomptant', but in process of time the word, which was always pronounced by dropping the 'p', became gradually changed both in pronunciation and in orthography to its present form.

    a. AIG
    b. ABC Television Network
    c. AMEX
    d. Accountant

30. The _____ is the global organization for the accountancy profession. IFAC has 157 member bodies and associates in 123 countries and jurisdictions, representing more than 2.5 million accountants employed in public practice, industry and commerce, government, and academe. The organization, through its independent standard-setting boards, establishes international standards on ethics, auditing and assurance, education, and public sector accounting.
    a. International Accounting Standards Committee
    b. Emerging technologies
    c. American Payroll Association
    d. International Federation of Accountants

31. A _____ is a type of debt Like all debt instruments, a _____ entails the redistribution of financial assets over time, between the lender and the borrower.
    a. Debenture
    b. Lender
    c. Loan to value
    d. Loan

32. _____ is the term used to refer to the standard framework of guidelines for financial accounting used in any given jurisdiction. _____ includes the standards, conventions, and rules accountants follow in recording and summarizing transactions, and in the preparation of financial statements.

Financial accounting information must be assembled and reported objectively.

a. Long-term liabilities
b. General ledger
c. Current asset
d. Generally accepted accounting principles

33. The term '_____' refers to the concept of collecting information and attempting to spot a pattern in the information. In some fields of study, the term '_____' has more formally-defined meanings.

In project management _____ is a mathematical technique that uses historical results to predict future outcome.

a. Trend analysis
b. Regression analysis
c. 3M Company
d. Multicollinearity

ANSWER KEY

Chapter 1
1. d   2. c   3. d   4. c   5. c   6. d   7. a   8. c   9. a   10. d
11. b   12. b   13. d   14. d   15. a   16. a   17. a   18. d   19. d   20. a
21. b   22. d   23. c   24. c   25. c   26. d   27. d   28. d   29. d   30. b
31. c   32. c   33. d   34. d   35. c   36. d   37. a   38. c   39. b   40. d
41. d   42. d   43. d   44. d   45. a   46. a   47. d   48. a   49. b   50. c
51. d   52. b   53. a   54. d

Chapter 2
1. c   2. b   3. d   4. d   5. c   6. d   7. d   8. d   9. d   10. d
11. d   12. d   13. b   14. b   15. a   16. d

Chapter 3
1. b   2. b   3. a   4. d   5. c   6. c   7. d   8. d   9. a   10. c
11. d   12. b   13. d   14. b   15. d   16. d   17. b   18. d   19. d   20. d
21. b   22. b   23. d   24. c   25. d   26. d   27. d   28. d   29. c   30. d
31. b   32. c   33. d   34. a

Chapter 4
1. d   2. d   3. d   4. d   5. d   6. a   7. d   8. a   9. a   10. c
11. d   12. d   13. a   14. d   15. c   16. d   17. a   18. d   19. d   20. d
21. a   22. a   23. a   24. d   25. b   26. d   27. d   28. a   29. d   30. b
31. d   32. a   33. d   34. a   35. d   36. a   37. d   38. d

Chapter 5
1. c   2. d   3. b   4. d   5. b   6. d   7. d   8. d   9. d   10. b
11. a   12. d   13. b   14. d   15. a   16. d   17. b   18. c   19. a   20. d
21. d   22. d   23. c   24. c   25. c   26. d   27. d   28. c   29. d   30. b
31. b   32. b   33. b   34. b   35. d

Chapter 6
1. d   2. d   3. b   4. d   5. a   6. b   7. b   8. c   9. a   10. d
11. a   12. d   13. c   14. d   15. b   16. d   17. d   18. d   19. d   20. d
21. d   22. c   23. d   24. a   25. b   26. c   27. d   28. b

Chapter 7
1. d   2. a   3. a   4. d   5. d   6. c   7. a   8. d   9. d   10. b
11. d   12. d   13. a   14. d   15. a   16. d   17. c   18. d   19. d   20. a
21. a   22. d   23. d   24. d   25. d   26. d   27. b   28. d   29. d

Chapter 8
1. d   2. c   3. c   4. d   5. d   6. d   7. d   8. a   9. b   10. b
11. d   12. d   13. c   14. b   15. d   16. a   17. d   18. b   19. d   20. b
21. d   22. d   23. d   24. d   25. a   26. d   27. d   28. d   29. d   30. d
31. c   32. d   33. d   34. d   35. c   36. d   37. d   38. b   39. b   40. c
41. b

Chapter 9
1. d	2. c	3. d	4. a	5. d	6. d	7. d	8. d	9. a	10. a
11. b	12. b	13. a	14. d	15. a	16. c	17. b	18. d	19. c	20. d
21. d	22. d	23. d	24. c	25. d	26. d	27. a	28. a	29. d	30. b
31. a	32. d								

Chapter 10
1. b	2. d	3. d	4. d	5. d	6. a	7. b	8. d	9. d	10. d
11. c	12. b	13. a	14. b	15. d	16. d	17. d	18. b	19. d	20. d
21. a	22. d	23. c	24. d	25. b					

Chapter 11
1. d	2. d	3. d	4. a	5. d	6. d	7. d	8. d	9. d	10. d
11. d	12. b	13. c	14. d	15. b	16. b	17. c	18. d	19. d	

Chapter 12
1. c	2. d	3. d	4. b	5. d	6. b	7. d	8. d	9. d	10. c
11. d	12. d	13. c	14. d	15. d	16. d	17. b	18. d	19. a	20. d
21. d	22. d	23. d	24. d	25. a	26. a	27. a	28. b	29. b	30. a
31. c	32. d	33. c	34. d						

Chapter 13
1. d	2. b	3. d	4. d	5. c	6. b	7. d	8. c	9. d	10. c
11. d	12. c	13. d	14. d	15. d	16. d	17. b	18. d	19. c	20. a
21. a	22. b	23. d	24. a	25. b	26. d	27. d	28. a	29. c	30. c
31. d									

Chapter 14
1. d	2. c	3. c	4. d	5. d	6. d	7. d	8. a	9. d	10. d
11. c	12. d	13. b	14. d	15. d	16. a	17. b	18. d	19. d	20. d
21. d									

Chapter 15
1. d	2. c	3. d	4. d	5. c	6. c	7. d	8. b	9. c	10. b
11. d	12. a	13. d	14. d	15. a	16. d	17. a	18. d	19. d	20. d
21. d									

Chapter 16
1. d	2. d	3. b	4. c	5. d	6. d	7. b	8. d	9. b	10. d
11. d	12. b	13. b	14. d	15. c	16. d	17. b	18. c	19. d	20. c
21. d	22. d	23. b	24. d	25. d	26. c	27. b	28. b	29. d	30. d
31. d	32. d	33. a							

www.ingramcontent.com/pod-product-compliance
Lightning Source LLC
Chambersburg PA
CBHW082051230426
43670CB00016B/2858